MUSTARD
SEED FAİTH

MOUNTAIN MOVING IDEAS
TO **CHANGE** YOUR LIFE
BY CHANGING THE LIVES
OF **OTHERS**

ERIC HARRISON

DEDICATION

This book is dedicated in memory of my father Micky Harrison, whom I lost in July 2017. Not only did he always encourage me to write, but in dying, he taught me how to love and finish well.

TABLE OF CONTENTS

INTRODUCTION

Writing a book has been a dream of mine for most of my adult life. Since my grammar school days, I have enjoyed writing and expressing my ideas on paper, while being encouraged through the years by many people to do so. My greatest advocates have been my family—the most persistent being my father, whom I lost a couple of years ago. Thus, writing this book accomplishes a number of personal achievements.

Firstly, I am accomplishing a significant personal goal I wasn't sure if I would ever achieve, and secondly, because this book is a posthumous tribute to my father. He has influenced me more than anyone else ever has, ever could, or ever will. My father could bring me to stages of anger that were ugly and self-defeating, but he also could encourage and inspire me to unimaginable limits.

My dad was a mentor to not only me, but to many others as well. He could push us to be better than we ever thought possible. Almost always, when experiencing growth, we find ourselves hating the teaching but loving the results. My dad was that teacher to a lot of people, and anyone who knew him would tell you that he was the hardest on me. Looking back, I often hated him for that, but now, knowing his heart and intentions, I am aware that I am a better man because of what he did.

What I enjoyed most about my dad was that we could smile and laugh together—and we did that a lot. Oftentimes, it was at the expense of one another, but it taught me that, at times, I shouldn't take myself too seriously. As I write this book, I hope that my father is looking down from Heaven and smiling with me again. I know that publishing this book would have made him proud. So, Dad, this is for you.

At the outset, I proclaim, with no apologies, that I am a devout Christian. I am not the guy on the street corner yelling at people to repent, nor am I the guy who passes judgment on others because of their sins or the way they live their lives. Rather, I am a sinner saved by grace. As far as I understand the tenets of my Christian faith, in the eyes of God, sin is sin. This means that my sins are just as heinous as the foulest of sinners and, as such, I am in no position to judge anyone. In a world that is becoming more and more supercilious to different lifestyles, and ways of thinking, my job as a Christian is simply to love people. All people. The same way that sin is sin in God's eyes, people are people, and it is not my job to judge; that's His job. No matter how they define themselves or how they are labeled by society.

Do I believe that the Bible is true and within it there are scriptures that condemn certain actions, behaviors, and lifestyles? Yes, I do. But for a Christian man who has lived almost his entire life in the conservative Bible-belt state of Texas, I believe that my job is to love other people no matter what. Unfortunately, there are many misunderstandings of the Christian faith, and evidence continues to mount, illustrating that we are under attack from the current culture and mainstream media. And as a Christian, I have to admit that some of the blame lies directly with the Christian church.

My example of how I should live and relate to the world is exemplified in the life and legacy of Jesus Christ. Jesus lived in some tumultuous times, too; narcissism, misogynism, and racial profiling were just as prevalent then as they are now. As are all of the other current sociological and economical struggles our world is living with today. Yet, Jesus's desire was to meet people where they were and to show them the love of God. I contend that if more Christians were focused on delivering Jesus's example of love and peace, that the world would be a much better place. I would further argue that, just as it happened some 2,000-odd years ago, that our culture can be transformed today. Jesus didn't shy away from challenging cultural norms. In fact, he destroyed them one by one. He associated himself with people who society said were flawed, different, and, yes, sinful. And he did so to spread his message of love and hope.

This is not just another book about Christianity or spirituality. Yes, it is based upon the tenets of my faith and, more importantly, on the inerrant Word of God, but the difference here is that I intend to show you that our world is in need of new ideas, and new ways of thinking, just as it was at the time Jesus lived. Not only by Christians, but by all people living, working, and serving together for the greater good of everyone. The principles taught in the Bible are just as relevant for people who don't believe in it, read it, or know about it, as they are for those who do.

For those who pick up this book with no affinity with religion or the church, for those who have been offended or feel judged by 'religious' people, or even those who vehemently oppose the ideals of Christianity—I ask you to give this book and my message a chance. My mission is not trying to convert you or even getting you to agree with me, but what I will present to you is one Christian man's views that I hope are somewhat different and surprising, intending to encourage you to think differently about what a Christian is. This book is my apologetical approach to illustrate what I believe Christianity is supposed to look like, and why I believe that it can become a foundation to rebuild and transform the divisions within our society today, just as it did when Jesus began his earthly ministry. I truly believe that we are all more alike than we are different and if we impact one life at a time with hope rather than hate, then we will slowly, consistently begin to change the world.

I am appealing to people of all backgrounds and all nationalities to read this book, and to put into practice the bridge-building suggestions proposed within, for the future of our country and our world. I promise that if you read this book, you will feel compelled to be part of the solution rather than the problem. This has worked in my life, and I want to see it work in yours.

And finally, my last reason for writing this book is to encourage people from all walks of life. I want to be very clear that this is not a book about prosperity. My intention is not to say that if you are a good person, or that if you start reading the Bible, or become a Christian, that your life will be better than it's ever been. This is not the case, as we Christians manage doubts, struggles, fears, and sins as much as anyone else. However, my goal—to use a well-known proverb that Jesus used—is to encourage you that if you will take what you have, use it and nurture it every day, and not be dissuaded by any negativity or naysayers, then you will be infinitely more fulfilled.

This book has been organized into four sections, with three chapters in each. Within each chapter, I use three distinct concepts to amplify my ideas, and at the end of each chapter, there are three 'mountain-moving ideas' that I provide as suggestions for you to apply immediately. I believe that you will change your life if you take these suggestions and act on them immediately. It is also possible that you will develop a desire to change the lives of others.

My intention for this book is to encourage you to take action. If you simply read it and set it aside to go on to the next book, then I have failed in my overall mission to encourage you to change the way you think and act. I hope this book touches your emotions in such a way that it sets you on a new course, for these ideas are not meant as solutions, but rather as talking points to reassess where you are in your life. In fact, my intention is that you use them to grow your own ideas and actions. I hope that they birth things that

I have never thought of based on you taking them and implementing them with others.

To that end, I have included two free gifts at the end of the book as a thank you for purchasing, and also in the hope that it encourages you to take action. The first gift is a small group study guide. This should be used to encourage further conversations around the ideas in each chapter. The second gift is a short ebook intended to amplify and clarify why the BAM (Being Different, Acting Different, and Making a Difference) lifestyle is so important to me, and why I believe it can change your life by encouraging you to change the lives of others.

There are many mysteries in the Bible, and the parable of the mustard seed can certainly be classified as one of them. As you will learn while reading this book, Jesus tells us that with faith as small as a mustard seed we can accomplish amazing things. The message I hope to share from this book is that if you are willing to be a faithful, forgiving, and loving person, then you have the power to change your little corner of the world in ways that will be beyond measure. Interested? Intrigued? Ready? Good. Then, let's get started....

SECTION 1

THINKING
DIFFERENTLY

CHAPTER 1

TROUBLED TIMES CALL FOR RADICAL IDEAS

*"The revolution that's required isn't
a revolution of radical ideas, but the
implementation of ideas we already have."*

RUSSELL BRAND, COMEDIAN AND ACTOR

I am deeply concerned about the divisiveness that exists in the United States of America today. Certainly, we have had our fair share of conflicts, enemies, and wars with other nations and cultures in the nearly 250-year history of our nation, but never have we been in such radical conflict with each other than we are today. I was not alive during the World Wars, and I am too young to remember Vietnam, but I cannot imagine any enemy in our history who has been more vilified than people who stand in conflict of cultures and ideas in our country today. What founded, established, and endured to make this country the admiration of the world now threatens—and indeed in many ways already has—to split it into predetermined segments of society who are completely intolerant of opposing points of view. Rather than seeking to understand each other's viewpoints, we are now more concerned with voicing our own vitriol and sharing it within the groups we associate with.

While it is hard to imagine, the world just before the birth of Christ was in just as much turmoil as it is today. Corruption, slavery, bigotry, and sociological upheaval were only a few of the prevalent problems. While difficult to place ourselves in that type of agrarian economy, and to realize the struggles that many people faced in those times, it is, however, congruent with the oppression and struggles many share around the world today. With seemingly little hope for change, and against insurmountable odds, there came a Jewish carpenter whose radical ideas not only put him in direct conflict with the established ideals of the day, but also started a revolution that changed the world and continues to make an impact today.

I do not intend to write a book that attempts to push Christianity on anyone. I do intend, however, to present facts that I believe are instrumental in changing the way all people, and especially Christians, think and act. Jesus did no less during his time on earth. If we as a nation are ever going to become the *United* States again, then I believe we need to examine ways in which we can come up with new and radical ideas and mindsets to bring us together instead of driving us apart. There are no revelatory or new thoughts here, only a reminder of long- and well-established ideals that need to be remembered, and implemented, starting today.

Do not judge, lest you be judged.

We live in a country that is badly in need of reversing the way we view other people. Rather than casting a suspicious and scrutinous look upon others, we need to first look inward. Not only did Jesus say that we would be judged if we judged others, but he also said that we would be judged with the same measure. Yikes! Think about how the last couple of days, weeks, and months have gone for you. What kind of thoughts have you had about your family, your friends, and your co-workers? How about the person who cut you off in traffic, or the rude clerk at the coffee shop who didn't listen to you? And that is before I have begun to mention the person or people who have different views on politics, religion, race, gender, and sexual orientation.

I ask you: If you were judged by others with the same thoughts and words that you had used toward them, how would you feel? Going one step further, what if you had to live with the same consequences you had seemingly justified in your own mind that the people you judged should have to live with? Would that challenge you to reconsider how you look at other people, now and in the future?

How much better would your small corner of the world be if instead of adopting a mindset and mantra of judgment, you instead developed one of forgiveness? Do you think you would surprise a few people—especially the ones who know you best? You might not start a revolution, but you sure might find that your world, and the people in it, are a little brighter, a little happier, and a whole lot less stressful. Forgiveness is not an easy concept. As my father used to say, *"If it was easy, everyone would do it."* Unfortunately, the opposite seems to be true today: almost nobody does it.

Forgiveness requires humility and a mindset that must be adopted by us all if we are ever going to change our culture. Specifically, my challenge to you is to adopt a mindset whereby you never expect to get and never cease to give. You can insert any positive character trait that you want into that equation. In addition to forgiveness, you could also use righteousness, humility, grace, hope, and love. You may not always—or ever—receive them, but you should never cease to give them.

Look at the speck in your own eye.

We are all experts at defining problems, pointing out shortcomings, and giving corrections. Especially to anyone and everyone other than ourselves. We expend a great deal of energy every day worrying and working around the flaws we see in other people. Think about your conversations at the end of the day when you finish working—either with your spouse or with friends. Do you spend a great deal of time talking with them about what other people did that irritated you? We all do it, and it is a habit that needs to be broken.

Again, Jesus, in his teachings, reversed the societal norms and pointed out a new way of thinking. Both Matthew and Luke record Jesus saying, *"Why do you look at the speck of sawdust in your brother's eye and pay no attention to the plank in your own eye?"* Not only does Jesus point out that we must reverse the way we think about others, but he clearly offers a bit of rebuke for micro-analyzing flaws in others while ignoring significant flaws in ourselves.

The next radical idea suggested in the above statement is that we need to work on ourselves, and if we become better people, we will become the kind of person that others enjoy being around. In other words, if we fix ourselves and are working toward becoming the best version of ourselves every day, we spend a lot less time being hypercritical of others. We are likely to find that the more we work on ourselves, the more those around us will fall in line and do likewise. People who are self-confident and achievement-minded naturally inspire others to follow suit. I believe that if you work on yourself twice as hard every day, you will likely find that the problems you have with others will be cut in half, if not more.

The other benefit of being a better version of ourselves is that as we become better at being, we will become much better at acting and doing. We can all put ourselves in a negative reinforcing loop where everything we think and do pulls us down further and further. Ultimately, this can make us into more negative people. However, we can reverse the direction of our thoughts and actions, and make everything multiply in a positive way. Our world would be a much happier place if we all lived by the principles of multiplication rather than the negativity of division.

With all the division in our society today, there are a whole lot of people on both sides of any issue living with stress, clenched teeth and fists, and looking for a fight. It is virtually impossible to look at any form of media and not be affected by the venom pervading it. What if instead of clenched fists, we all started extending a helping hand? It could be something as simple as smiling and sharing a kind word with a stranger. But real change can come if we follow the advice of Stephen Covey, author of the iconic book, *The 7 Habits of Highly Effective People*, and *"seek first to understand, then be understood."* What amazing changes could eventuate if we simply relax and open ourselves up to listening and learning rather than yelling and lecturing?

I think the other message Jesus is telling us in this passage is that it is a mistake to project our reality onto others. We all have specks of sawdust in our eyes. We are all flawed human beings. We assume that when we see the speck in other people's eyes, we know why it's there, how it got there, and how to fix it. The truth, in most cases, is that we don't know the real reason why it is there. Especially when the people we are judging are outside of our circle of social, religious, political, or cultural circles—we have no idea what trials, tribulations, and tragedies these people have been faced with. We certainly do not live in a perfect world, and, as the saying goes, we all have our crosses to bear. The way we were raised, the circumstances we have dealt with in our lives, and the challenges that keep us up at night, are uniquely ours. Other people may have similar situations, but they are certainly not the same.

> **Let he who is without sin cast the first stone.**

As alluded to in the last section, I have some news for you: we are all flawed. While our society attempts to sell us on the idea that if we just work hard enough, own certain things, be identified with particular groups of people, and have enough followers on social media, that we will be set for life. The truth is that this is all a fallacy, as we are all imperfect and prone to mistakes in our judgments and actions. Perfection is a fleeting idea that we would all be wise to stop pursuing for ourselves and demanding from other people.

The story of Jesus challenging the teachers of the Law with the woman caught in adultery is a familiar one, even to those not closely linked to Christianity. The leaders were convinced that, according to the rules of the Jewish Law, the woman deserved to be judged and killed for her adulterous behavior. However, Jesus completely turned the tables on them when he challenged the first sinless person to throw the first stone, and as no one could claim they were sinless, they all slowly walked away—I imagine with them shaking their heads and muttering to themselves. Thereafter, Jesus is known to have asked the woman, *"Where are your accusers? Has no one condemned you?"* To which she then replied, *"No one, sir."* And Jesus said, *"Then neither do I condemn you."*

The point of the story is this: we are all sinners in need of grace. Yes, grace from God, but certainly also grace from other people. Recall earlier in the chapter where I encouraged you to always be willing to give, whether you receive or not. Grace certainly falls into this category.

I need to address something that I believe is very important for everyone in our society to understand. This is not just relevant to Christians, but people of all faiths, no faith, and people from all groups of societal, sexual, and political backgrounds. In the eyes of God, sin is sin. My sins as a Christian are no different than the sins of someone with no affinity or affiliation with the church. As a Christian, I do not see the sins of others as any more vile or worse than my own. Because my God does not. He did not come to divide us, but to unite us, and I believe that anyone who behaves or speaks differently is doing a disservice to the ministry of Jesus. Jesus did not come to divide us but to unite us.

Finally, I want to encourage my fellow Christians as well as those who are critical of the Gospel of Jesus that it is high time to 'step across the aisle,' and get to know one another better. We are much more alike than we are different; we are driven by the same desire for health, wellness, love, and joy; and we want to create the best versions of ourselves and make the world a better place to live in. I truly believe that most people have an inherent desire within them to be and do better. Let's put aside the differences that divide us and focus on the words, actions, and behaviors that will multiply the goodness we all seek.

It's a radical idea—but just the right kind of radical idea needed for troubled times.

FOR REFLECTION
THREE MOUNTAIN-MOVING IDEAS

- Keep a daily journal, and each day record how much time you focused on working to better yourself instead of focusing on other people's faults. You should be spending twice as much time on yourself.

- In the same journal, and with the same goal ratio in mind, estimate and record how much time you spent that day on giving instead of getting.

- Identify two to three random acts of kindness that you can do <u>every day</u>. It doesn't have to be grandiose or life-changing. Most Random Acts of Kindness can be quite simple but still have a profound impact on the receiver.

CHAPTER 2

RADICAL IDEAS CHANGE CULTURE–AND HISTORY

*"Change your thoughts and
you change your world."*

DR. NORMAN VINCENT PEALE, MINISTER AND AUTHOR

At this point in the book, I hope to have received the attention of more than just Christians. My aim is not to write a book that 'preaches to the choir' but to write a book that a) changes attitudes about Christianity, and b) changes Christians' attitudes about our society. This chapter is addressed to my Christian brothers and sisters, so if you are not one of 'us,' please hang in there with me until the next chapter. All that said, it is more than okay to take the message from this chapter because, while it applies primarily to people of the faith, as with all the words and lessons of Jesus, it is also intended for those who question his motives and authority.

Love your neighbor as yourself.

For those of you not familiar with these words of Jesus, let me briefly explain. Jesus was questioned by one of the experts in the Mosaic Law. The question was what Jesus would say was the greatest of all the commandments. His reply was *"To love the Lord your God with all your heart, mind, and strength."* Then he uttered the words that absolutely stopped those who had heard him in their tracks: *"The second most important command"*—after loving God— *"is to love your neighbor as yourself."* The apostle Paul, in his letter to the church in Galatia, took it a step further when he wrote, *"For the law is fulfilled in keeping this one command: love your neighbor as yourself. If you bite and devour each other, watch out or you will be destroyed by each other"* (Galatians 5:15–16, New International Version).

In the time of Jesus, the term neighbor has been widely debated, but in understanding the Bible, you must understand the culture that Jesus was immersed in. In twenty-first century terms, the word neighbor means essentially anyone and everyone that crosses your path. It could be the person sitting next to you on the airplane, the 'crazy person' cutting you off in rush-hour traffic, or the person on the street corner begging for money. No matter the circumstances, no matter the location, no matter the length of time with which you interact with someone, *everyone* that you meet during your day should be considered your neighbor, based on the definition that Jesus gave. So, yes, that means that every single person you see, touch, or talk to, deserves to be loved with the same love you have for yourself; and for Christians that also includes God. After all, according to scripture, we are all created in His image.

I can't help but think of the Golden Rule when I consider the challenge to love other people the same way that I love myself. If I am to truly get into this mindset and imbibe this into my life, I understand that I must reverse my thinking to incorporate the idea of treating others the same way I wish to be treated. It is easy to say, but in practice, it is really a challenge because some people are hard to love, and others we would just as soon avoid rather than interact with, much less love them with an all-consuming and selfish love that we have for ourselves. However, if we're truly going to change our culture and make a positive impact on the world, this will be our challenge.

We all make plans, whether they be what to have for dinner tonight or what goals deserve our focus and best efforts, and we quickly become self-absorbed and focused on ourselves and what we need and want. What if, instead of putting our needs and wants first, we took into consideration how we could take others along with us for the ride? What if, instead of building fortunes and accumulating toys for ourselves, we set out to think about how we could use our gifts to benefit others? Ponder this for now, but I will discuss more about this in the next chapter.

Finally, I would like to encourage you to be aware that the only way to love others well—as we are commanded by our Lord—is to get real and get small. What do I mean by that? I mean that we must consider others before we consider ourselves. The true measure of a woman or a man is how many people they lifted on their way to the top. If you are accomplishing your goals at the expense of other people, and the highway of your success is littered from the fallout of building yourself up, you have made yourself much more important than you need to be. In the grand scheme of things, all your wealth, all your possessions, and all your accomplishments mean very, very little. What will matter in the end is who you took with you, who you loved well, and who you benefited along the way. And the answer shouldn't be a few people; it should be all your neighbors.

I have come that they might have life and have it abundantly.

Many of us that are unfamiliar with Christianity, and even some of us who are immature in our faith, stumble over these words. They do not mean that if you are or become a Christian, that you will be magically transported out of your present circumstances and have the perfect life with no pain, sorrow, or worries. Instead, these words mean that becoming a Christian should change your perspective on how you look at everything. For example, this includes how you view people that are outside of your normal socioeconomic circles and believe differently than you do. The abundant life changes everything.

I believe we are facing a great epidemic in our culture whereby we are all burrowing ourselves into our own little groups fraught with a scarcity mentality. For example, 'Only *we* can be part of our club, and if you are not a member, there is obviously something very wrong with you.'

This idea of scarcity is also transferred to how we manage our lives, as we are scarce with our resources, our time, and our talents. And if we share our resources, time, or our talents, we reserve them only for the select few who happen to view the world the same way we do. Jesus's culture-changing ideal is that we should live our lives with an abundance mentality, that we should share everything and reach across boundaries to people from different religions, genders, races, and political views—even when we don't agree on everything. We should be celebrating our differences, rather than using them to build walls around ourselves.

Let's be clear: abundance is for everyone. It is all our responsibility—devout Christians or devout Atheists, and anyone in between. We all need to take care of our planet, to reach out to the oppressed and the poor, and to comfort those in need. It is impossible to study the life of Jesus without drawing the conclusion that he lived by reaching out to others by sharing abundantly. Wherever you are, with whatever you have, it is your responsibility to reach out and serve those around you. Joyfully. And with an abundance mentality.

I have had times in my life where I have been primarily secluded and disconnected from the outside world, groups of peers, friends, and others. I have also had times in my life where I have related to groups of people doing exciting things. When I am engaged in activities that make the world a better place, and where I am making a positive difference in the lives of other people, the person getting most of that benefit is me. If you have never experienced this before, I cannot encourage you strongly enough to get yourself involved with a group of activists making a difference in the world. It might be a church group, a service organization, a group of friends, or a Toastmasters club. No matter what it is, there is a special jolt of energy that comes from helping and supporting other people, while working with other like-minded people. Such groups change cultures, and history.

There is one word that Jesus used a lot that, in my opinion, is one of the most overlooked words of his ministry that is applicable not just to Christians, but to all of us. And that word is...*go*!

Again, I am speaking not just to my Christian brethren but to all of you: get up and go. Put actions to your thoughts, dreams, desires, and words. Be a person who makes things happen, who makes an impact and leaves a mark. It may be exhausting at times, or you don't feel like it, or you may see things in other people that make you feel angry, hopeless, and sad. But it is better to live a life running the gamut of emotions and experiences than living a life of regret. So, my advice to you is: *go*!

Abide in me.

One of my favorite chapters in the Bible is John chapter 15. Within this chapter, Jesus says, *"I am the vine and you are the branches."* He goes on to tell us, if we abide in the vine through obedience to his word, that we will bear much fruit. This may seem somewhat of a foreign concept to those not familiar with his teachings, but once again, let's look at how his message is relevant to all people.

The first requirement to bear fruit is to stay connected or plugged into the source. We'll dive much deeper into how seeds and trees get their nutrients and grow in the next section of the book, but for now, suffice to say that if a branch becomes disconnected from the vine, it will wither and die.

A former pastor of mine, Dr. Jim Denison (denisonforum.org), gave me a great analogy a long time ago that has stuck with me all these years later, which helps amplify the message of this passage. If you look at a power drill, it is an amazing tool. With it, you can build any number of things that can serve yourself and others in many useful ways. You can build a fence, a bridge, a boat, or a car. But the drill has one very important thing that renders it useless if you are ever without it. What is it, you ask? It's a power cord.

If a drill is not connected to its source of power, it is completely useless. We, too, especially us Christian folks, are useless to the world around us if we are not connected to the source of our power, Jesus Christ. I hope Dr. Denison will forgive me if something got lost in translation, but don't you just love that analogy? It certainly has made an impact on me since I learned it nearly twenty years ago.

Next, if we can learn to abide in Jesus, we will soon discover that all we really need can be found in him. I have reached a point in my life where I have learned that what I need is truly a lot less than I initially thought it was. Ninety-nine percent of what I really need is family, friends, faith, and health. Sure, I enjoy some of the finer things of life just like everyone else. I also have an affinity for the outdoors, especially if I can play golf and have a good meal with family and friends as well.

It took me many years to discover a lesson I wish I would have learned in my twenties or thirties. As the old saying goes, when God is all you have, God is all you need. The things that we chase after are fleeting at best. I guess, as my children lovingly say now, I have become an 'old geezer.' I accept that title, and say to those of you in your twenties and thirties: take care of the few things in life that you really need, so that when you are older, they will take care of you. If more people lived by this principle, our culture would be radically changed for the better. Don't let the 'stuff' of life cloud what is clearly most important.

This leads me to ask the question, who (or what) is your focus? Try this exercise. In the last hour, estimate how much of your time you spent thinking about or interacting with yourself versus thinking about or spending time with other people. My guess is that, if you are honest, you spent a minimum of forty-five minutes (75 percent) of your time thinking about yourself. Next, make it your goal to spend 50 percent of the next hour focusing on others. Then try to completely reverse it in the next hour and give 75 percent of your efforts to others. This is a simple exercise that, with time, will change the way you think and act, and make you a much more de-sirable person to be around. The kind of person who will positively impact all sorts of people, including those who are different to them. Indeed, this is how the first-century church was born, grew, and remains relevant today.

Finally, in this chapter of the Bible, Jesus clearly states, *"I have told you these things so that my joy may be in you and that your joy may be complete."* I just gotta say: *wow!* Why would I not want to stay plugged into this source? Complete joy? Sign me up! This is a bold statement, just as many of Jesus's statements are, but this one is at the top of the list in my book. In a world filled with hate, anger, bigotry, abuse of all kinds (and we're not even talking about politics yet), you're telling me, Jesus, that I can have complete joy?! It's a bold statement and radical idea that was big enough to change culture and history 2,000 years ago. And, I can say with utter confidence because of what I have experienced in my own life, that Jesus is 100 percent correct. You may find it difficult to believe, but I challenge you to put Jesus to the test.

FOR REFLECTION
THREE MOUNTAIN-MOVING IDEAS

- Journal and/or brainstorm at least eight to ten very tangible, yet relatively simple ways that you can implement the golden rule into your daily Life beginning now.

- Take some time to reflect and meditate on whether you find it simple or difficult to practice an abundance mentality. Think about why that is. What one or two key changes can you make to change from a mindset of scarcity to a mindset of abundance?

- Research and identify three to five local opportunities that match up with your passions and your skills, to get involved in and determine where you can find ways to 'go'!

CHAPTER 3

WHAT IF...?

———

*"Imagination is the beginning of
creation. You imagine what you desire,
you will what you imagine, and at
last you create what you will."*

GEORGE BERNARD SHAW, PLAYWRIGHT

When writing the message in the last chapter, I got excited. I hope I inspired some ideas within you, too. To close out this section, I challenge you all to take action on your thoughts, to be people who don't just think good thoughts but who go out into the world and accomplish great things. People who get out of their comfort zones, face their fears, and make changes within their circles of influence that make the world a little bit better, and a happier place to be. As I said earlier, we are all much more alike than we are different, so let's put down our biases, our acrimonious war of words, our judgmental attitudes, and then come together to make positive changes.

I imagine that some of you are now scoffing and making excuses as to why I am a dreamer, delusional, or just plain wrong. I accept your criticism. And if you decide to take no actions, I admit that in many ways you may be right, and I will be wrong. But I would rather be in the minority of those trying to make positive changes than among the majority that sits silently on the sidelines and complains about every which thing, but refuses to do anything to change their position for the better.

> **Lift others more than you promote yourself.**

I am beginning this journey with the goal of one revolution. For now, I am just one, but I hope to add many recruits in a short period of time. The first and most significant thing I am looking for are people who are ready to get uncomfortable. People who are not afraid to confront things that may have caused them fear, anger, or resentment for most of their lives. And of course, I am also challenging my fellow Christians, but this is also a call for all people from all walks of life.

To put it simply, we must get out and meet people where they are. In a society that is more concerned about their profiles and the number of likes they receive on social media compared to reaching out to their neighbors, this calls for a radical shift in our thinking. I am convinced that our lives, our communities, and our country would be so much better if we would just reach out and help those who need it. Obviously, there is a lot of work to be done, and I am not promoting an agenda here, but rather a mindset that the best way to set things on the right track is to form relationships with a number of different people and offer to help. It is not about promoting yourself, your religion, your agenda, or your ideals. It's simply about caring—caring for people. Is that so hard? And if it is, I challenge you to evaluate why that is, and reset your goals to focus more on other people than on yourself. Achieving goals that benefit other people eliminates division in our society, thus multiplying the effect of your efforts. And we'll explore those benefits momentarily.

The primary obstacle to overcome is the one between our ears. Many of us accumulate as much 'stuff' as we possibly can with no concern for who we had to step over to get it, and without a desire to share it with anyone. In my life, I have accomplished many, many things that I am very proud of. However, the truth is, there is virtually nothing I have ever accomplished in these moments by myself; whether it was the love and support of my wife and family, or the tireless efforts of people on various teams, I would be hard-pressed to think of a major accomplishment I have earned totally by myself. However, I know there are a lot of brilliant people in the world that are a whole lot smarter than I am, and who have accomplished amazing things all by themselves. While I am certainly impressed by these people, I believe it must be lonely at the top if they never got to work with others or share the benefits of being part of a team.

I have also been associated with, and been a fan of, some great teams over my lifetime. I may be biased, but celebrating victories with, and for, a team, are some of the major highlights of my personal and professional career. I know that I would much rather be part of a team that ascends a high mountain than walk up a hill alone. Therefore, I challenge all of you—whether you are young and just starting your career and family, or whether you are an empty nester preparing for the twilight of your life and career—to seek to achieve every mountaintop experience you can. I assure you that your life will be enriched—and not just because of the journey, but because of the people that you will take with you along the way. You will be forever grateful that you brought them along!

The next challenge I pose is a request that you stop trying to be the problem-seers and instead start to become the problem-solvers. There are unlimited opportunities right outside our front door just waiting for some caring, concerned, and committed people to solve them. Some of them might be solved with almost no effort at all, but others might take years and require thousands of man-hours and dollars. The good news is that there are many community, civic, and government organizations already set up to deal with the greatest needs of our society. But the biggest problem most of them have is the lack of people and resources available to accomplish their objectives. Again, what if we all became more concerned about other people and became problem-solvers rather than problem-seers? How much more neighborly would our cities, towns, and communities be?

Finally, let's discuss the idea of turning division into multiplication. It is much more than a play on words; it refers to thinking seriously about how to reverse the negative energy in our country. Rather than focusing on our differences, why can't we focus on what our common interests, desires, and outcomes are? When this country was founded, it became the envy of the world because although we were all different, we all worked together, accepting each other's differences, and creating a place where dreams come true. When we focus on what divides us, our dreams turn into nightmares, and we certainly have a few that we need to work through in our country. In just the same way I've outlined above, we can reverse the direction on the path we are currently headed and, one by one, start to change the conversations, attitudes, and actions we take toward others to once again make this the land of opportunity. For everyone.

From clenched hands to open arms.

Let's talk about how we act, as well as how we think. Instead of walking around amped up and looking for a fight, what if we were to go around looking for opportunities to embrace others, and lift them up so they become the best versions of themselves?

Call me a sap, a romantic, or even a lunatic if you want, but I don't think there is anyone in this world who doesn't love a big, warm bear hug. There is something about a hug that is open and vulnerable. It removes not only the walls that we build around our physical bodies, but also within our mental makeup. Is it just me, or does it seem like hugging has become a more prevalent act in our society? Maybe the 'bro hug' between men has dropped barriers that existed for a long time, but I have heard more people—men and women—in the last several years, say almost apologetically, *"I'm a hugger."* Where did this come from? It is my belief that as our society has become more and more divisive, our needs for genuine human interaction—and yes, embracing—has increased.

I believe that not only are we all starved for attention as a result of the 'screen time' age, but that people have a need and a desire to express their emotions, which have become way too suppressed. I Invite you to drop your guard every now and then and experience the pleasure of a warm, open embrace. It may feel a little uncomfortable at first, but I assure you that it is much more comfortable than walking around with a critical attitude and clenched fists.

It is also important to evaluate what your overall vision for your life is. What and who you worship becomes your master. The world already has enough people who are out to get and consume everything they can with no regard for others. If, however, you are a person who cares about other people, then I believe that you and others like you can make a significant difference in our world. The question that we should all be asking ourselves is who are we doing this for? Only you can answer that. Fill in the blank with whatever you're doing at any moment of your day; who and what is it for? If you're undertaking an act for others, then a lot of people will be glad to meet you.

In addition to who you are working for, I would ask you to consider what your legacy will be when you are gone. Are you leaving a trail of tears, and the skins of everyone you have slain along the way, or are you leaving behind a better world because of the people and organizations you positively impacted while you were here?

It's an important question that I ask myself often. It is also a tenet of my Christian faith, and one I hope we can all use to positively influence others to follow suit because of the good they have witnessed from our actions.

Finally, in a world ready for a fight, who have you shocked lately? As mentioned above, I love the idea about random acts of kindness. These ofttimes small and simple acts can change the course of the person they are given to as well as make the giver feel better about themselves. Our world is filled with a lot of discord, hate, and stress right now. A simple smile and a 'hello' could be just what a stranger in the morning coffee line needs to hear. It could be as simple as a phone call to someone you should have called last week, or a note to an old friend. Because I believe our culture is starving for genuine, heartfelt, human interaction.

If you put enough random acts of kindness together, you will very soon become a person who makes a difference in your world as well as someone who 'delightfully' shocks other people. In a world in need of good news, let's make our headlines make a positive difference for a whole lot of people today.

As I have loved you.

I believe that the statement above is one of the most overlooked, yet important messages that Jesus ever said. Many people who are unfamiliar with Christians, or our doctrine of faith, mistakenly assume that being a Christian means being a boring, rule-following, life-sacrificing martyr. Worse yet, is where we are seen as judgmental, narrow-minded, and intolerant. What I would like those who have wrongly judged us to know is that nothing could be further from the truth. The author of our faith (Jesus) did not live his life in this way, and he did not command his disciples to do so either. I believe the words of Jesus above, and, hopefully, his message in the following text will change the minds of the harshest critics of people who follow him.

First, let's put the entire passage in context before evaluating what many Biblical scholars think Jesus meant by them. In chapter 15 of the Gospel of John, verse 12, Jesus says,

> *"This is my commandment, that you love one another as I have loved you."*

It is also worth noting that in the next verse Jesus adds,

> *"Greater love has no one than this: than to lay one's life down for his friends."*

This sounds strikingly like our earlier discussion about loving your neighbor as you love yourself (whereby you determine that everyone is your neighbor). In other words, Jesus did not say: love other Christians and judge everyone else. Hardly at all. In fact, with the same love in which we say sinners are saved by grace, we should all love other people in the world. It is just that simple.

Anyone speaking on behalf of the Christian faith that says or acts in a way that shows judgment or bias, in my opinion, is not living in accordance with the faith they proclaim. I am not trying to minimize anyone's beliefs or convictions, but I must say that I believe much of the conflict between Christians and society is due to the fact that we are not living in concert with Jesus's charge in the preceding verses.

Also, as noted before, my sins, and the sins of all Christians, are no different than the sins of any other person or group of people with whom we share a difference of opinion. The simplest, most succinct way I can summarize this for my faithful friends, as well as those who believe we are the problem and not the solution, is this: our job is to love; God's job is to judge. Period.

If we do our job and do it well, then love wins. Every time. Hatred and differences simply cannot stand up to it. If we rightly love one another, then we will continue to see that love 'won' another. It is not a trick, creating a diversion, or being manipulative. If love is the basis of all that we do, as He has loved us, then no negativity, criticism, or animosity stands against it. We win, everyone wins, and love wins.

Next, let's talk about loving other people that think and act differently than we do. This is one of the hottest topics facing our world today—diversity, of any and every kind. Sexual, racial, gender, religious, and whatever else you'd like to add. In an effort to be transparent, while hoping I do not open myself up to being thought of negatively by others, I have a confession to make: I am a difficult person to love. Why, you ask? Because I am a messed-up, selfish, and self-centered person. Just like you. But you know what is really cool about me? And you? We're all really messed up. We all really need help, and love, and grace, etc. etc. The good news for the two of us, and the rest of the messed-up people out there, is that we are loved by the God who created us. And that applies to everyone in the world, regardless of their sexual orientation, race, religion, or creed. I hope you agree that is really exciting news and worth sharing with everyone. It is much more important to recognize the similarities we all share rather than comparing where and how we are different.

Jesus did *not* say love one another as I have loved those who follow me, or those who keep my commandments, or those who attend my church. He said, very clearly, love one another as I have loved *you*. That means that the next person I see, and every next person thereafter for the rest of my life is loved by God. Just like I am. Pretty cool, don't you think?

To wrap up this section of the book, I want to reiterate one more time that as Christians we should have no biases toward others, and no judgment when it comes to other people's beliefs or lifestyles. We are all free to live our lives without the burden of worrying about how other people live theirs. The better we do the latter, the less the former will matter. And the more attractive we will be to other people.

It is clear that there is a lot of work to do and a lot of damage to be repaired, but the question of this chapter is the question that was asked 2,000 years ago when it changed the world: What if? It may not solve all our problems, but it sure might build a superhighway that enables us to get to our destination a lot quicker.

FOR REFLECTION
THREE MOUNTAIN-MOVING IDEAS

- Evaluate your goals—past, present, and future. How many of those goals directly benefit others instead of being focused on you and what you want?

- Brainstorm and record the actions you need to take to change from a problem-seer to a problem-solver. Share them with someone you trust and who will hold you accountable.

- What attitudes, acts, traits, or characteristics will you adopt to become more loving and less judgmental? Clearly define what success in this area of your life looks like.

SECTION 2

A PARABLE
OF FAITH

CHAPTER 4

MUSTARD SEED FAITH

"Discipline is the soul of an army. It makes small numbers formidable; procures success to the weak, and esteem to all."

GEORGE WASHINGTON, FIRST U.S. PRESIDENT

I n this section and chapter of the book, we turn our attention to one of Jesus's many well-known parables. Jesus often taught using earthly, common things well known to those who listened. Within them were messages with a much deeper meaning, and principles that were more important than what appeared on the surface. This message was not intended for only his followers, and today, this is a message for all people, regardless of their beliefs or lifestyles. In the parable we will examine in the next few chapters, I will qualify what I believe is Jesus's successful life formula for all people.

Let's read Jesus's parable of the mustard seed and examine what it is, discuss what lessons he intended us to glean from it, and assess how it should impact our daily lives. Although this parable is recorded in three of the four Gospels, I am referring to the passage in Matthew 17:20:

(Jesus) *replied, "Because you have so little faith. Truly, I tell you, if you have faith as small as a mustard seed, you can say to this mountain, 'Move from here to there,' and it will move. Nothing will be impossible for you."*

I will briefly explain why the verse began with Jesus pointing out that the disciples had so little faith. The disciples had just experienced one of the most incredible personal and religious experiences of their lives, as Jesus had called them to a mountain and transfigured into a holy figure before them. Immediately after this experience, and coming down from the mountain, they were approached by a desperate father who recognized them as disciples of Jesus.

Suffice to say, these men came down the mountain with their feet a few inches above the ground because of their incredible interaction with Jesus. But as they descended the mountain after their unforgettable, life-changing experience, they were immediately met by a man with a young, demon-possessed son who begged them to remove the evil spirit. Despite their continued rebukes and futile attempts, the three disciples were unsuccessful.

Some time later, Jesus arrives on the scene. I imagine he was thinking to himself, *"Really, guys, did you not learn anything when we were up on the mountain a little while ago?"* He immediately rebukes the evil spirit, and it departs the young boy. When they questioned Jesus as to why they were unable to do it, he points out that the reason they struggled was due to the fact that they had so little faith. Thus, we arrive at Jesus's teaching of possessing 'Mustard Seed Faith.'

Plentiful, well-known, ordinary.

Jesus spoke of a mustard seed, which was something very common in the first-century agrarian economy that he lived in. Everyone would have known exactly what he was talking about when he mentioned a mustard seed. He wasn't asking anyone to reach beyond their means to comprehend the deeper lesson he was trying to communicate. Not only was a mustard seed very ordinary, but it was also very plentiful. Like mustard seeds, we all are uniquely different; however, in so many ways, we are all the same. There are a lot of us that have the same thoughts, ideas, dreams, and goals. We all start out with the same opportunity, but some of us flourish, some of us struggle, and some of us get eaten up by the weeds in our lives.

My encouragement and motivation for you is equally simple. We all have the potential to achieve great things, as does every other person on earth. Think about your mentors, role models, and the people you admire and aspire to be like. They are just the same as you and I, but they have figured out to take what they have been given, and with a determined and consistent effort, turn opportunity (or small seeds) into great accomplishments. Whether you are just getting out of the starting gate in your life, career, marriage, etc., or whether you are entering the twilight of them, it is never too late to start multiplying your efforts. For this will only multiply your results in a short time.

Jesus encouraged his disciples to consider that opportunities in him are unlimited, and that if you exhibit just enough of the right kind of faith, nature will provide the right kind of resources to ensure your mustard seeds grow into flourishing plants and even larger trees. If you doubt either of these principles, I challenge you to put them to the test. Both require a small amount of faith combined with the actions needed to nurture growth. We have to look beyond today's realities to see tomorrow's possibilities.

There is a clear correlation between faith and action in any realm. In the agrarian realm, before nature can do its work, the farmer must nurture the seeds. In the relational world, you hope that if you're a nice person, your love interest will be attracted to you. This requires you to work on the relationship. In business, it is the same, as sales and profits come from a lot of hard work that the end-user of the product never sees. This is just so, in the spiritual realm, for we cannot hope that just because we want good things that they will just happen like a genie granting all of our wishes to come true. We have to have faith, we have to understand the reason for our faith, and we have to nurture it, so it continues to grow. Just like anything else, if faith is not growing, then it is dying from lack of commitment.

So, given the above, my friends, the first lesson I want to draw our attention to regarding the parable of the mustard seed is that it is up to us to put the extra in the ordinary. Jesus did not say if you hope things will go your way, you can do amazing things. He also did not say that if you're a good person, tell the truth, and love America, then everything will be okay. He said the first thing we must do is act. Just a small, tiny mustard seed of a little extra effort to turn your life into an extraordinary adventure.

Daily discipline.

To overstate the obvious, if we are going to truly move mountains, we can't just try once or twice, and if nothing works, then simply give up. Anything worth achieving and having requires us to undertake the work that needs to make it happen. Every day. Often, the work is mundane, and our efforts seem to largely be a waste of time and energy, but then all of a sudden one day, *wow*! All our hard work pays off and we quickly forget the hard work it took to get there. But if we are going to become people who achieve great levels of success in any endeavor, we must do the work with diligence and determination. The time we invest today will often pay major dividends tomorrow.

The more committed we are to achievement, the easier it becomes to show up all day every day and make things happen. Many high achievers swear that it only takes a little bit of extra effort to cross over from someone who does things to someone who gets things done. Once you start the momentum going in a positive direction, it is almost impossible to slow it down. They want to do and accomplish even more, and the momentum increases exponentially the farther they go. Of course, as I have seen, the reverse is also true. I bet you've seen it, too.

I encourage you to become a high achiever. The ones I know, myself included, swear by holding themselves accountable to written goals, which they review and act upon daily. While most people will say they have goals, according to success leader and coach Brian Tracy, the best research estimates that less than 3 percent of Americans have written goals and less than 1 percent review, rewrite, and act upon them daily. I hope that the inspiration from this book and the lesson from this parable challenges you to raise that percentage, and thereby raise the probability that we can make a positive impact on our country or small corner of the world.

I love the quote by Mr. Motivation himself, Zig Ziglar, *"If you don't pay the price for success, you'll pay the price for failure."* Truly, each day we all must make a choice whether we want to pay now or pay later. Sure, you can eat donuts for breakfast and pizza and ice cream for dinner every day. You may be incredibly happy while eating it, but tomorrow you may be overweight, feeling sluggish, or on your way to becoming diabetic. To bring it back to the parable, if you're going to move a mountain tomorrow, you best be working on your plans and your faith today.

Finally, allow me to take my 'old geezer' perspective and remind you that time is precious. When we are first starting out, it seems as though time is never-ending, but our time does indeed slip away too quickly. My point is, don't have the mindset of as soon as _____ happens, then I'll get to that task or idea. Or once I get _____, then I will set aside time to work on _____. Ladies and gentlemen, life is uncertain. I hope and pray that your runway stretches well into the future, but the truth is we live in a world where tragedies happen far too frequently. This is your time: today. This is your chance to live and embrace every moment because not one of us knows when our time on earth will be over, and all those things we thought could wait for tomorrow will never be accomplished. Too soon, tomorrow becomes yesterday. I encourage you to consider that anything you might not want to do today will not hurt you nearly as much as regretting you didn't do it tomorrow.

> **A desire to do or be something more.**

Faith, by definition, is a belief that is not based on proof. I have faith that if I work hard and run a principle-based company, that I will make enough profit to support myself and my family. However, the reality is that businesses—and very good ones—can still fail if we fail to pay attention to the key performance indicators that make the business viable. I have faith that when I turn the key in my car, the car is going to start. My point here is that even though we don't know the intricate details or understand how or why things work, we just trust that they will. Although I cannot prove beyond a shadow of a doubt that things will go exactly as planned, I live under the assumption that they will. That is faith in its rudimentary form. Faith is lived moment to moment and proved over time.

I believe that faith is born out of a desire to have a mindset that lifts ourselves and others up to higher desires, loftier goals, and greater achievements. There are plenty of skeptics who like to share that certain things cannot be done, but our world is often defined by people who accomplish amazing feats because they have a higher belief—or faith, if you will—in themselves, and what they believe is possible. In order to have faith, it is not necessary to be a spiritual person; however, faith traces its roots directly to the belief in, and devotion of, God. It looks past beliefs, achievements, and status quos to ascertain possibilities that could lift ourselves and the world we live in.

I want to encourage you again, if you are not already, to become a person who sets and achieves goals. I do believe that, by and large, most people have an innate desire to do well and be well. I would caution us, however, that as the oft-quoted saying goes, *"The road to hell is littered with good intentions."* We may very well have some great ideas and plans for how to get there; and if we work hard enough, we may eventually arrive. But accomplishment comes from doing the things every day that allow us to reach our destinations we seek for the long term.

I grew up in a time where we didn't have Google Maps, Garmin devices, and Waze. If you wanted to plot a trip across town or across the country, you had to refer to a road map or an atlas. No matter what tool you use today, if you use a map, you will be aware of the length of the journey and arrive much more quickly while knowing where you are in relation to your current progress before you get there. Start revising the maps you need to get to your desired destinations today.

Next, let me ask you to consider whom you will be taking with you on these road trips? This is just as important as where you are going because, when you consider (besides you) who will benefit from achieving your goals, this leads you to your Whys. Your Whys are the motivation that keeps you pushing ahead when everything seems to be telling you to stop. If your goals are the engine of your life, then the Whys are the fuel making the engine go. In other words, in addition to yourself, who are the happiest people in the world going to be that you persevered and accomplished your goals?

Finally, when considering goals and how to achieve them, make sure your planning is circular, and not linear. What am I talking about? I believe, along with almost any other goal achievement guru I have ever read, that you should have goals that affect every area of your life. For example, your personal, professional, spiritual, social, and economic roles, to name a few. The more you attach goals to these key areas that deserve your attention, the more well-rounded you will become.

What does all of this have to do with Mustard Seed Faith? We'll explore that more in the next chapter, but just know that with a little extra effort, you can accomplish anything. Just like anyone and everyone else has done since the beginning of time.

FOR REFLECTION
THREE MOUNTAIN-MOVING IDEAS

- What one or two seeds can you plant today that could grow into huge possibilities tomorrow?

- Will you commit today to become a member of the 1 percent who sets, monitors, and works daily to achieve your goals?

- Set aside time this week—a few hours to half a day—to clearly identify your whys.

CHAPTER 5

TINY SEEDS

---

*"Work is doing it. Discipline is doing it every
day. Diligence is doing it well every day."*

DAVE RAMSEY, AUTHOR AND RADIO HOST

B efore we get too far ahead of ourselves discovering together
what Jesus was trying to teach us from this parable, let's first
examine one of the key components of the story: the mustard
seed. I have read several critics claim that Jesus was wrong about
the mustard seed being the smallest seed. However, I think Jesus's
point here (and mine, too) is to appeal to his audience. As previously mentioned, Jesus took an object that was indeed one of the
smallest seeds but, more importantly, was well known and readily
available in Israel both then and today.

The agricultural community in which he dwelled would have understood that a mustard seed can quickly grow into a huge tree in
a very short period of time, not the small mustard plants that we
are familiar with in this part of the world today. More on that in
the next chapter. Let's take our little mustard seed and use some
analogies to analyze his parable. This also solidifies my message of
inclusion and to show that every life matters to God and should
matter to us, whether we believe in Him or not.

Seeds to sow.

In our lives, we have all been given gifts, whether we recognize them or not, whether we are using them or not, and whether we have perfected them or not. I believe every single person was put on this earth for a special reason and purpose. Obviously, Jesus espoused this message throughout his ministry, but, my friends, let me tell you that no matter who you are, where you are, and what you have or haven't done up to this point in your life, *you* still matter! For there is only one of you.

One thing that Jesus taught that I wish more Christians would talk about outside of the walls of the church is the fact that God doesn't see us as we are today. He sees what we can become in the future. Just like the mustard seed that soon turns into a big tree, so do you have the potential to rise up and achieve things that only you were uniquely created to accomplish. Friend, I believe you have the potential for an incredible future if you take hold of your dreams and become who you were created to be. Unfortunately, far too many of us spend most of our time thinking about what we've done instead of what we need to do. I want to challenge you to spend at least twice as much time thinking about what you can do, rather than what's already been done. What an exciting future we would all have and what a positive world we would all live in if people were to adopt this new mantra!

When it comes to planting seeds, whether you know anything about farming or gardening, or if, like me, you know virtually nothing at all, generally everyone can agree that the more seeds you plant, the more you will have to harvest. Obviously, not every seed you plant turns into a big, beautiful bush, tree, or flower. So, we plant in rows knowing that the odds are that at least some, if not most, of what we plant will soon reap a harvest. The same is true with your seeds. It's not just a one-and-done effort. Therefore, make sure the seeds you plant are not only well planned, but also cover a fair amount of ground. That way, even though some of them may not bear fruit, you are sure to bear some.

It's important for me to note that some people naturally have more seeds to plant than others. Some of us have been blessed with enormous 'crops,' while others have very meager means and barely get by. Once again, my friends, in the eyes of God, and in my way of thinking, whether you have an acre of seeds or one meager seed, each one is valuable in God's eyes. One seed can become one enormous tree, so if you only have one seed to sow, then plant it, nurture it, care for it, and watch what your efforts can turn it into with the help of the Master Gardener.

When considering how to best sow your seeds, it is important to recognize that there are times when you need to sew diligently, but there are also times where knitting comes in handy, too. Let me be very clear, I have never sewed or knitted anything in my life.

The reason I mention sewing and knitting here is because there are a couple of important distinctions to make that apply to our discussion. When you sew, you can bring together multiple inputs and create something much bigger than originally planned. It's a process that requires a fair bit of planning, focus, and concentration. When you are sewing, you are best to be completely focused on the task at hand.

Knitting, on the other hand, is a much more tedious, yet somewhat relaxed activity. In knitting, you have largely only one input, and while it requires a lot of tedious work, it can be done at a very leisurely pace and accomplished while doing other activities, especially interacting with and relating to others. I mention this because there is a time to sew, and a time to knit. Both have to be done, but one cannot dominate the other. Whether you're sewing or knitting, your goal should still be on producing a finished product. That is, the more you focus on your goals and evaluate your efforts, the more likely you are to accomplish them.

How healthy is your soil?

I do not profess to have any gardening or farming knowledge whatsoever, but I think that even the most novice among us knows that if you are going to plant seeds and reap a good harvest, the most important thing you need to start with is healthy soil. I will not pretend to compose a cognizant approach to creating good soil. I just know it helps to have it.

Of course, throughout the world, and even in different regions of the United States, we have all kinds of soils where certain types of vegetation, plants, and flowers thrive. So, the good news is that wherever you are, if you take the soil you have and make it as healthy as possible, your chances for success are pretty good. But before you plant, you only have one chance to ready the soil that you will plant in, so it is wise to ensure the soil is as healthy as possible. This is because you can change a lot of inputs once the planting has begun, but what you can't change is the soil. Likewise, you only have one chance at this life, so put your best foot forward and make it count. You can take as much time as you want to get your soil ready, but at some point, faith takes over and you must start planting. In your life, be sure you don't wait too long to start planting. You may never be totally ready, so you must step out in faith and observe what your soil will produce.

As you prepare your soil and try to make it as healthy as possible, consider if you are going to use fertilizer or manure. I realize that, by and large, they are the same thing, but in our world there are innumerable resources you can use to help your soil (life) flourish. With all the information we have available, even on our smart-phones, we don't have to look far to find resources that we can use to help us grow and thrive. Unfortunately, the opposite is also true and often a good bit more pervasive. I caution you to watch what you're putting into your soil—make sure it is quality fertilizer and not a poor substitute that ultimately stunts your growth.

Although there comes a time to step out in faith and start planting, I wish to caution against not preparing well. You must till your soil until it is fertile, ready to receive what you will plant. Many of us are guilty of rushing ahead and jumping in headfirst after a new, shiny object; however, make sure that you are aware of whether you are waiting too long to plant or planting too early. Both could yield the same disastrous results.

I can't talk about fertile soil without thinking about water. Nothing on earth can survive without the proper amount of water. Some of the most important charitable organizations in the world are those that are striving to get clean water to areas that do not have access to it. Clean water brings health, reduces disease, and gives life to everything it touches. As a Christian, I cannot help but think about my need for the Living Water that is provided to me every day through Jesus Christ. To be clear, I am referencing Jesus's example in the Bible given to the Samaritan woman at the well where he compared the water we drink, and yet thirst again, with the Living Water he offers, which forever quenches our thirst. I have made it my mission, with this book, and with my life, to do whatever I can to enable that water to flow through me so that everyone who's affected by me gets to access pure, clean water that gives abundant life.

All the same.

To conclude this chapter, let's focus on the message that each and every one of us has been given a gift of seeds to sow. Maybe you only have one, or maybe you have enough to supply a small country. Whatever you have been given, I want to encourage you to use it for good, and not just for yourself, but for everyone that you can impact. Who knows how big your seeds might grow, and how vast an area your crops might cover? Without question, if you never plant your seeds, the world will miss out on what you could have done to make it a better place.

To use a baseball analogy—we all start at home plate. We all have the same chance to come to bat and take our swing at life. Even the best baseball players in the world hit the ball 30 percent of the time. But when they do get a hit, the whole game changes; then opportunities abound everywhere. Suddenly, the game gets much more exciting, and the team must use strategy to try and take advantage of the opportunities to produce a win for the team. Sadly, some people are afraid to come out of the dugout and take a swing. Don't let that be you. Sure, you may strike out nine times out of ten. But while you'll be faced with a lot of disappointment, you'll never miss out on the thrill of that one hit.

Let's take the baseball analogy one step further. Once you have made the decision to get up to bat, don't be tentative. Walk to the plate with confidence, get well positioned in the batter's box, and be ready to swing with all your might. Some people finally get off the bench and come up to bat, but they're so tentative, they just meekly stick their bat out, hoping the ball might make contact and they can sneak their way onto the bases. I say, the heck with that. The world is waiting for confident people to come up to the plate and swing for the fences. Everybody loves a home-run hitter. And oh, by the way, every home-run hitter uses every strikeout to increase the probability that the next time they come up to bat, the ball is leaving the yard.

I cannot emphasize enough the most important lesson I take from thinking about every mustard seed. They are similar in their initial appearance, as they all start out with virtually nothing to distinguish them from any other seed. But God wants everyone to know that each seed, each life, has been created with a unique and special purpose. A small number of select people become well known for what they accomplish in their chosen fields. Some become renowned within the communities that they live in for how they act and treat people. The vast majority of us, however, languish in obscurity and seemingly have very little impact. I believe that if you take your tiny seeds and use them as I have suggested, then you will discover your unique and special purpose—and be so glad that you did. As will everyone that is within your circle of influence.

Finally, let's conclude this chapter with an emphasis on how every life matters. Every sex, race, religion, political party, and socioeconomic group matters, and there is no one in this country or the world who does not matter. If you take issue with this statement, especially if you are a Christian, I challenge you to examine yourself and spend time in meditation contemplating how you could draw any other conclusion.

I will close with a message that I hope resonates with those outside of the Christian faith: Jesus taught, the Christian Church confirms. And I, as an aging, white, Christian male living in the Bible belt, reaffirm that each and every person in the world matters, and that in the eyes of God no one is more or less valuable than anyone else. Jesus shared this as a message of hope, grace, and reconciliation. I offer it to anyone and everyone, and again encourage people of all faiths, or no faith at all, to set aside your biases and recognize that we are all created in the image of God.

FOR REFLECTION
THREE MOUNTAIN-MOVING IDEAS

- Set aside time to make a list of all of the things you would like to accomplish before you die. Dream *big!*

- Evaluate your current efforts. Are you waiting too long to plant, or rushing to plant too soon? What things do you need to change to ensure a healthy harvest?

- Put yourself in the midst of the baseball analogy. Are you coming up to the plate, excited to use your skills, or are you hiding in the dugout? How can you become more motivated to better yourself and to help others?

CHAPTER 6

HUGE TREES

---

*"Someone is sitting in the shade today because
someone planted a tree a long time ago."*

`WARREN BUFFET, BUSINESSMAN AND PHILANTHROPIST`

I f you research mustard seeds and the trees they produce in
Northern Africa and the Middle East, you will find that they
are different to the small yellow mustard plants than we see in
the United States. I contend Jesus used the analogy of the mustard seed because his hearers would have known that though tiny,
within five to ten days, these minuscule little seeds would sprout
and grow into some of the largest trees within the region. In other
words, to loosely summarize Jesus's teaching in this parable, consider my submission: *"Take the smallest thing you can think of, take
care of it, and you will soon see that it will produce a huge result."*

Just as the little mustard seed, seemingly overnight, becomes a tree
that grows a minimum of twenty feet high. A tree of this size
changes the landscape all around it, becoming a source of life and
energy to everyone and everything who sees or touches it.

Multiplication.

This is not a book on business or finance; however, I want to introduce you to a financial term that I have created. I guarantee you will want to incorporate this into your life and attempt to increase its value. This special measurement is the 'Return on Daily Effort' or RODE. There is a very explicit formula that you need to follow in order to make your RODE pay off.

First, you must make daily investments. That sounds easy enough; however, the catch is that for several days, weeks, months, or years (depending on how big you want your tree to be once it is fully grown), you will see absolutely no results from your efforts. However, if you are willing to be patient, the formula will be working behind the scenes. It will appear that all your efforts have yielded nothing, and then all of a sudden, seemingly out of nowhere, your tree and whatever that represents, will grow exponentially larger and faster than you can imagine.

In Darren Hardy's book, *The Compound Effect*, he eloquently explains how over time, through daily investment, you will begin to see your investment grow exponentially. I encourage us all to consider a mindset of multiplication rather than division. Consistent daily effort, plus time, equals multiple benefits for everyone, and rewards your consistency and determination.

Additionally, consider any and all acts of kindness, and charity or investing, as a long-term process. It is my belief that our culture and society is in direct opposition to this stance. Our culture says, *"It's all about me; I want it now, and I will not wait."* But I encourage you to go against that mindset. In other words, achieve the little things every day that, when compounded, will pay off much bigger in the future. You will not get rich quick, but your life will be richer. And we could all use some lessons in delaying self-gratification and spending what we have today on benefits that will pay more richly in the future.

I would like to again mention the positive reinforcement loop. I am a big sports fan, and, in the thousands (although my wife might argue the millions) of games I have watched over the years, no matter how good or how bad the teams might have been, there is nothing more exciting than when Big Mo comes to visit your team. Who is Big Mo, you ask? Well, sports fans, Big Mo is momentum. For there is no denying the feeling when your team seizes the momentum in a game. Once achieved, it seems nearly impossible for the opposing team to reclaim it. Unfortunately, the reverse is also true, for if Big Mo decides to go to the other side of the field, you're in big trouble.

The point of analyzing positive momentum is to seek to do whatever you can to seize it. Every little win leads to a bigger win and more momentum. The easiest way to start your day with positive momentum is to build little wins into your routine at the start of every day. It may be as simple as making your bed in the morning or developing a morning routine of prayer, meditation, and exercise. The more you make winning a habit, the easier it is to achieve even bigger wins. Eventually, winning becomes a habit. It may take some time to get there, but once you're there, it's awfully hard to get knocked off your perch. I highly recommend you make Big Mo one of your best friends.

I hear some of you saying that Big Mo doesn't exist. Breaking out of a losing streak is almost as tough as keeping a winning one. For every team that achieves historical success, there are five times as many that do not. You may feel like it's time to just give up, throw in the towel, and not put forth any more effort because it's just too hard. I have been there, and I sympathize with you, but I will tell you—whether you are a young struggling entrepreneur or a seasoned veteran who can't seem to find his next career opportunity—it's always too soon to stop trying.

To achieve Big Mo, you must believe in yourself and in the multiplication process. It may take more time and effort than you think you have, but I promise you that if you work at it every day, the wins will begin to add up and you will see your future suddenly burst forth with new opportunities. Just like that good old mustard tree.

Pruning to bear more fruit.

When it comes to growing big, healthy trees, just about everyone knows that if trees are going to thrive, they need to be pruned. If we put our lives in the place of the tree, we go through a period of pruning ourselves many times over. It is often times painful, and we may not see the reason for it, but the arborist or the one who knows more about you than you know yourself, is aware that it is absolutely necessary to make cuts today in order to produce better fruit tomorrow. For those of us who have had parts of our lives (limbs) cut off at various times, we know how painful this can be. At that moment, the event usually makes little sense, and we are saddened and angry for our loss. Only with time and perspective do we realize that the cut, while painful, was necessary to produce something even better in our lives.

In order to survive, a branch must stay connected to the base or trunk of the tree. The branch gets all its nutrients and water directly from the source—the trunk. This analogy is the same in our spiritual lives. If we do not stay connected to the source of our strength and growth, we quickly wither and fall prey to the smallest of life's storms. Even those who rely on a source other than God for their strength and vitality will encounter the same issue. If you rely only on your own abilities while not caring for your body, then you run the risk of losing your effectiveness, if not your ability to survive. In and of ourselves, we cannot survive alone. Physical health requires food, proper diet, and exercise, to name a few. Mental health requires proper respect and care for yourself and others. And so on.

You may not like it; you may have had your world turned upside down by it; and you may be angry at yourself, others, or God about it, but I would bet that the pain you have endured thus far in your life has been for a reason. Sometimes the reasons are very difficult to understand. Especially when really bad things happen to really good people. It just doesn't make sense and makes you ask: Why?

However, my main point is that the smaller prunings in life—and although they hurt, they are not devastating—should, in the end, produce more fruit. As the saying goes: no pain, no gain. If you are going through a season of being pruned by life, instead of responding emotionally and angrily, try instead to note the pain, accept the circumstances, and ask yourself and God, why? Likely, the answers will not come quickly, but if you stay focused and alert, they will likely come sooner than later.

Whether you are a parent, or have only been parented to this point in your life, you will be familiar with the idea of discipline. Speaking as a father who has raised two boys and a girl, I can tell you that disciplining children is one of the hardest roles I had as a parent. In the end, I was a pushover, and my wife was the disciplinarian. And who do you think knew that more than anyone else in the world? My kids. Somewhere between my thirties and forties, I unsuccessfully vacillated between trying to be a parent while at the same time trying to be a best friend. I do not recommend this as a parenting strategy for raising teenagers.

However, I am much better at disciplining my children now. This took me a long time to learn, but when you discipline your children, you are showing them that you truly love them. I could write another book about all of the kids that came in and out of my kids' lives over the years. I could also meet other kids and tell you within seconds which ones had discipline at home and which ones didn't. It took me a while to get there, but one of the best things you can do for yourself and others is to show them discipline. It's not easy, and you will not be very popular at times, but it is absolutely worth it. A perfect example of this is where you may say no to a small reward today so that tomorrow a bushel of fruit will come forth.

And most importantly, at harvest time, once fruit gets ripe, you better eat it quickly or else it will spoil within a very short time. The kind of fruit we are looking to grow is the kind of fruit that lasts a lifetime and beyond. The kind you can leave behind that others can enjoy. Fruits like love, joy, peace, patience, kindness, goodness, faithfulness, gentleness, and self-control. These were the fruits the Apostle Paul wrote in Galatians that were gained by being filled with the Holy Spirit of God.

A benefit to everything it touches and everything around it.

When your small seeds finally become big trees, whether you are aware of it or not, you have done more for the greater good of your community and all of mankind than almost anything else you could do. Just like us, trees come in all shapes, sizes, and origins. Some trees are small and provide just enough shade for a few people who would otherwise have none. Some trees are so big that they impact the whole world. No matter how big or how significant it becomes, don't let yourself become complacent when it comes to growing your tree. There isn't another one like it. That's a promise.

There are several ideas that come to mind when it comes to planting and growing trees. No matter the derivation of your tree, it will still provide shade and support for everyone who is near enough to experience it. Maybe its impact is not something that is ever realized outside of a handful of people or a small community, but, nevertheless, without your tree in place, and without the support and significance of it, the world would miss out on what you could have done had you planted and nurtured.

One of the most exciting things about some trees is that as they mature, they produce seeds that can be regenerated and provide even more opportunities for the communities and countries where they take root. Some new seedlings are able to be transported across countries or around the world to make a difference far and wide. In a way, I hope we never really get to see the full impact of the work we do while we are here on earth. Nevertheless, it is an important question to consider, what will you build with the trees you grow? Some will be used to build momentous things that bless hundreds of thousands of people all over the world. Others simply reach out to impact a few people in need right where they are. No matter how big what you build becomes, trust the sowing and reaping process to the one who said, with the small seeds from which they came, you can move mountains.

I want to address some of you who again may be skeptical and critical of the whole notion of planting trees at this point. I hear you saying, *"There are trees everywhere; why do I need to worry about planting another one? Besides, if I did, with my luck, it would probably get eaten up by bugs and die anyway."* Well, Ms. Gloom and Mr. Doom, let me say to you that in the grand scheme of things you might be 100 percent right. The world is certainly not going to miss one more tree. We can justify just about anything in our minds. I've never seen a tree that didn't provide shade, and I've never seen a tree that a bird couldn't land and rest in and maybe even build a nest. So yes, your little tree may mean nothing in the grand scheme of things, but to the one person who needs shade or the one bird that needs a nest, your tree may be all they have.

Let me close our chapter and section by making clear that my point is not to plant and sit back and admire and brag to others about what an incredible tree-grower we are. Our world needs a lot more people who will plant seeds and nurture them and then let nature, and God, have its way. As the old Greek proverb says, *"A society grows great when old men plant trees whose shade they know they shall never sit in."* You may be neither old, nor a man, but what an incredible feeling to know that you left a mark, you made a difference, and you planted a tree that will live way beyond your time on this earth.

That's the kind of life that I want to live. As a Christian, that is the kind of life that Jesus challenged me to live. As a resident of arguably still the greatest country on earth, it is my responsibility to make a difference to as many people as I can. I hope you will join me in that pursuit.

FOR REFLECTION
THREE MOUNTAIN-MOVING IDEAS

- Are you striving to get rich quick or live a rich life? What will you change to become more patient and effective?

- Where and how in your life are you currently being pruned? How can you use this time to bear more and better fruit in the future?

- How good are you currently at disciplining yourself? What activities, people, or resources could help you improve?

SECTION 3

GROWING
AND MOVING

CHAPTER 7

SMALL FAITH

---

*"The smallest seed of faith is greater
than the largest fruit of happiness."*

HENRY DAVID THOREAU, ESSAYIST

I n this section of the book, let's dive into the parable of the Mustard Seed Faith and examine its components. We will also continue applying principles and ideas that can transform your life and, more importantly, transform our current culture.

The first aspect of the parable, obviously, is faith. There is a lot of talk about faith in our culture today. Unfortunately, in my opinion, much of this talk and much of the things that we are putting faith in are way off base. To name a few of the most popular ones, we put faith in our status on social media, we put faith in our appearances, and we put faith in our ability to handle all the 'stuff' in our lives. The problem with this is that all these issues are focused on self. Sure, there are other outside influences we put faith in, like the latest technology, a fad diet, or a shiny new object. These kinds of things divert attention away from your own reality and become the 'attraction du jour' to keep us from being real and honest with ourselves and others.

Real, genuine faith, as I understand and believe it to be, is the recognition that I am flawed and I need help. I need to believe in something bigger and better than myself. I can't keep living the lie that if I am good enough, everything is going to work out okay. Obviously, I hope to influence you toward a faith in God. However, if that is something you are diametrically opposed to, I will not try to change your mind, but I will show you what that looks like so you can come to your own decision.

> **Nothing more than the desire to change.**

If you are living in frustration and thinking negatively about the state of your life and our culture, you are far from alone. There are plenty of outlets and resources readily available to feed your negativity, and to convince you that our culture is in a downward spiral that is impossible to pull out of. Unfortunately, many of these outlets believe that people of faith are part of the problem, rather than the solution.

Whether you are a person of great or no faith, I purport that we all need to stop focusing on what is wrong with ourselves, our culture, and our country, and instead focus on how we can make a positive difference. If you are living a life that is unsatisfactory, and you are disgusted by the division you see around you every day, I want you to know that change can happen very easily. Acknowledging a desire to change is the biggest hurdle. I don't intend to oversimplify; however, a small mind change often leads to personal growth.

Let me encourage you with an example from the Bible that has always somewhat amused me. It is from the book of Acts, chapter 26, verse 14. This is the story of when the Apostle Paul was converted to Christianity by the voice of God. God says to Saul (his Hebrew name before conversion), *"It is hard for you to kick against the goads."* I must admit that I had no idea what a goad was until I looked it up. This is yet another example of the Bible using something that would be easily understood to the people that originally wrote and read it. A goad was a spiked stick used to help drive cattle. So, in effect, God was telling Saul in today's language, *"Dude, are you nuts? Stop kicking a stick with spikes and let that stuff go."*

Friend, if you've been living at the end of your rope for so long that all that's left is a few tattered threads, then I want to encourage you that there is a better way. This negative mindset can affect anyone in any circumstances. I know, because I was there for many years of my adult life. The damage I did to myself, my family, and others is one of my biggest regrets. Therefore, heed my advice—you do not want to live with regrets, so pull yourself up and make a new plan.

I can also tell you from experience that you can transform your life from one of frustration and anger to one that redirects your mind to focus on new ideas and new outcomes. No, this is not a story of *"I found the Lord"* because I have been a Christian since I was ten years old. It's about resetting your mind to set yourself up for success rather than failure. It sounds easy enough, unless, like me, you have years of practice finding reasons to be miserable. So although this change in mindset is simple, it's not easy, and it is all about being disciplined and committed. This is not only a theme to grow your mind as well as your life in every facet, but also a key to growing your faith.

Take any person who you admire for their accomplishments in their field. It could be an actor, a writer, a professional athlete, or a self-made entrepreneur who became a billionaire. I can guarantee that if you could meet any one of those people and ask them how they became so successful, they would tell you that, yes, they have some natural ability, but the main reason they became the 'best' at what they do was through hard work and dedication, which allowed them to become the best version of themselves every day.

Finally, I cannot say it any more plainly than John 3:30. If I really have the desire to change, the determination to make it stick, and the ability to see things differently, then *"I must become less, so that he can become more."* My friend, the world does not revolve around you. The less you focus on yourself and the more you focus on other people, the more your faith is going to increase, the more joy you are going to experience in your life, and the more that people are going to enjoy being with you. I speak from experience, and have benefitted from the results.

> **This is your time. This is your chance. Live every moment. Leave nothing to chance.**

Before you read another word in this book, I want you to make a commitment to yourself to stop living an unsatisfied life. I am not going to give you a blueprint on how to do that; I'm just telling you to do it. I want you to take out a piece of paper, and in your own way, and in your own words, make a commitment to yourself that, starting today, you are going to start living differently. Be specific and define *what* you're going to do, *how* you're going to accomplish the goals you've set for yourself, and most importantly, *why* you're doing it, *who* can help you do it, and also who will benefit the most when you accomplish them. Go ahead. I'll wait.

Did you get it done? Good. Do you feel excited about it? If not, go back, rethink, and rewrite them again until you are really excited about them. Take as long as you need to get this done, but don't stop until you get it right. When you're finished, come back here. However long it takes, I don't want you to miss this critical step.

Congratulations, my friend. You have just discovered the sure cure for the blues. There have been a million songs recorded and a fair number of books written about the blues and how to overcome them. I am not suggesting that you are going to find your answer in—or through—some other object or person, as the only person who can decide if you are going to reclaim your life and, ultimately, your legacy is you. There are plenty of resources to help you if you need them, but you are the only one who can decide if this is your time. Make it count.

Here is even better news: if you change today, tomorrow is going to be even better, and the day after tomorrow is going to border on awesome! It is the law of the positive reinforcing loop. Stack enough good days, one after the other, and you get to the point where you are more prepared, opportunistic, and excited about tomorrow.

Now, instead of being downcast and focusing on everything that is wrong in your life, you are now hopeful and looking for opportunities to do more and help more people. This is one of my big Whys for writing this book, as I hope it can help as many people as possible recognize that they have the ability to make a positive difference in their corner of the world. This mindset will also help others to develop and grow their faith in themselves and others, and especially in their creator. This is the way to true significance. I have seen it happen in my life, and I want to see it happen for you. Do not waste another day or another opportunity to rise and shine. Do it wherever you are, and do it now!

> **It's not the size of the mountain;
> it's the size of your faith.**

Thus far, we have talked about a small, mustard-seed-size faith. Since Jesus made it clear that even with a tiny bit of faith we can move mountains, it stands to reason that if our faith grows bigger, that, over time, it becomes pretty sizable, until with the right amount of faith, we could change the world! I really believe this is true, and if enough of us will buy into this line of thinking, it could happen very quickly. If a lot of people with a little faith got together and multiplied their efforts, I see no way it couldn't happen, and I have enough faith to believe that.

Often, the first step is the hardest: being bold enough to start and taking that first step, even if you're not quite sure where you're going. And once we get past the uncertainty of that first step, we're almost unstoppable. It's like watching a toddler learning to walk. At first, they are hanging on to what is secure with all their might, gently rocking back and forth. Then one hand comes loose and they experience more wobbling. Then, they let go with their other hand, and this turns the solid ground into a surfboard. Finally, that little foot slowly, meticulously, comes off the ground and, boom! That first step has been conquered!

But what happens after that? Sometimes, they fall to the ground, only to stand back up, but this time with even more confidence to take that first step, the second, the third, and so on. What happens then? The momentum overtakes them, and even though they're not quite in control, they are going forward faster and faster, usually with a smile on their face and with everyone else in the room cheering them on. So I say: go for it! The first steps are scary, but they lead us to places we've never been before.

Just as with the story above, change starts by taking baby steps. We're not sure of where we're going, or how we're going to get there, but soon we find new places, new adventures, and new opportunities we never knew existed. That one step will lead to more, which will open all kinds of new doors that lead to greater opportunities, and this will make huge changes in ourselves and the world around us.

The next challenge becomes identifying and focusing on your targets. In today's world, it is very easy to lose your focus and divide your efforts into too many projects. This makes you ineffective. True effectiveness comes from concentrating on a small number of targets. Culture-changing people of faith are individually focused on being the best at what they're good at, rather than running around ineffectively trying to do, and be, everything at once.

I recommend finding a tool such as StrengthsFinder™ (available on gallup.com), or other similar online tools to help you identify your highest, best uses so you can then find ways to use those gifts to make the most effective impact with your time. The goal is to *"Do whatever your hand finds to do and do it with all your might,"* as recommended in the Bible. If you are working from a position of strength, this is easy to do.

Finally, when it comes to faith, consider the question of what, or who, are you putting your faith in? As you think about this question, I challenge you to consider: Is it sustainable? Does it express a message and method of hope or hate? Is it moral? Do their core values line up with yours? Is it something that can and should be shared with others? I could go on, and so can you. The point is, as you drill down on these questions, you will soon realize that there are very few people or things that are worthy of putting your trust in. As a Christian, I know of only one—God. Our message of being loving and accepting has become distorted in our current culture. And unfortunately, some of it is based on the behavior and actions of some Christians who put the focus on themselves rather than the tenets of their faith. I challenge you to do your own research, ask all of the right questions, and see if any of your sources of faith can check all the boxes. Again, I strongly believe there is only one answer, and that is a life committed to living out the principles that Jesus taught and lived out.

As I close this chapter, I challenge you to examine your faith very seriously and sincerely. For, as illustrated in Jesus's parable, faith is very powerful. It can also be powerfully destructive, especially if you are putting your faith into the wrong things or people. Take some time with this, maybe a few days or a couple of weeks, as it is an important decision that deserves a great deal of thought. Especially if you intend to move mountains.

FOR REFLECTION
THREE MOUNTAIN-MOVING IDEAS

- What 'goads' in your life have you been kicking? What path(s) to success do you need to explore instead?

- Write your plan to begin living differently. then read it again to make sure you are clear on what you want to do and why.

- Identify three to five first steps you can take in the next thirty days to dramatically improve and impact your life. Break those down into weekly and daily goals.

CHAPTER 8

DAILY NURTURE AND CARE

*"We are all gifted, but we have to
discover the gift, uncover the gift,
nurture and develop the gift, and
use it for the glory of God and for the
liberation struggle of our people."*

LOUIS FARRAKHAN, MINISTER

It would be easy to skip over this chapter, or, for that matter, I could edit it out. However, it is prudent to consider what needs to happen behind the scenes in order to obtain mountain-moving results. This chapter will clarify how to nurture the soil of our minds and hearts to make the jump to significance from small beginnings.

It would be nice if we could decide one day that we are going to live a life that amazes even ourselves—and I hope many or most of you will—but it takes thought, it takes preparation, and it takes work. As anything that grows must be cared for daily in order to become the best version of itself that it can possibly be.

Do it today. Do it every day.

We've already discussed the need to stay committed and disciplined to working daily on your goals until they become a habit. As mentioned, often the first step is the most difficult. Many of us have the absolute best of intentions, but, for some reason, days turn into weeks and then into months, and we never get started. Our best intentions are just daydreams until we put some action behind them. Certainly, writing this book could have become that for me. I had help and encouragement from many people, but it still came down to me to take some action, as only I could sit down and start putting pen to paper and then fingers to keyboard.

While it is often difficult to start, once you have, and once you make it part of your daily routine, it's equally hard to stop. We are all, to some degree, creatures of habit. Seasons of life come and go, and our needs and desires change with them over time. Nevertheless, that which is most important to us must become routine.

Therefore, I encourage you to stop waiting for the right time, the right place, the right amount of money, or any other excuse you're using and start working on becoming the person of your dreams. The sooner you start, the sooner you will get where you want to go. It sounds like child's play, and it is, but so many of us take far too long to get started. So, don't wait, get started, and don't stop. You can do this, and once the feelings of accomplishment take over, you will not hesitate to do the thing that has become your most exciting goal.

After figuring out what you need to do, and what you need to get started, you then need to have some measurements to ensure it will help you reach your goals and measure your success. I am a firm believer in the old saying of, "*What gets measured, gets done.*"

Perhaps it's my competitive nature, but give me a firm number I am trying to achieve, improve, or attain, and I am all over it. If it is something that is just a 'would be nice to' or 'maybe someday,' then guess what? I am going to find one hundred other things to occupy my focus and attention. I bet you will, too.

Work your goals and objectives down to quarterly, monthly, weekly, and daily goals. No matter what you're working on. Before writing this book, I started out with a goal for total word count. I decided how long I wanted to take to write, edit, market, and finally launch my book. Although the ultimate goal was my launch date, at any point in the process, my daily word-count goal ensured that I knew whether I was ahead or behind schedule. You can set similar parameters with almost any goal, desire, or objective you seek to accomplish.

Achieve in threes. What the heck does that mean? To me, it means systematically breaking down my intentions, ideas, and goals into the three most important things. Goal-setting systems or planners can provide you with ideas on how to create and work on several goals. No matter what you are doing, and how you are doing it, I have found over the years the best way to be most effective is to look at what your top three priorities are. It can be for any period of time, from one day to one year. For example, what are the three most important things I need to do next week to bring me closer to becoming the person I want to be?

Once you have achieved those three things, then you can work through your other tasks, perhaps reprioritizing those into the next three most important things. The point is you're always working on the three most important things that are going to deliver the most value to yourself, and others, and bring you closer to realizing your dreams.

If you are not a planner or not an organized person, this may sound daunting, but trust me, you can do this with daily discipline and commitment. Once you do, you will wonder why you waited so long. You will also be more effective than you have ever been before.

Change is slow, until it isn't.

Just like watering seeds in a garden, many days and sometimes even weeks go by, and it seems as if nothing is happening, nothing has changed, and the fruits of our labor will never pay off. And then all of a sudden, just when we're ready to throw in the towel, we start to see little buds emerging from the ground. And before we know it, the little buds are big plants, and big plants start to bear fruit. This also applies to any goal worth accomplishing.

While there are varying reports, most experts agree that it takes about sixty-six days to form a new habit. That's just over two months. When you're taking on something new and uncomfortable, sixty-six days can seem like forever. Oftentimes it is. If you're going to truly transform your thinking and your actions and go from seeds to significance, there are no shortcuts. There are few people in life who become culture-changing individuals, and then there are the majority who start and stop, over and over again. It isn't easy, but the rewards are enormous.

The best advice I can give you on how not to become overwhelmed by the task before you is to put in the work until it becomes a habit. As there is no substitute for hard work all day, every day. And the secret to not becoming overwhelmed by the daily work is to plan ahead, depending on the goal—sometimes in months. Set targets, achievements, and accomplishments you want to hit for a month, a quarter, or a year. If you're focused on those more achievable goals, the daily work becomes more targeted, and you will be able to measure your progress over a longer period of time. This ensures you do not get distracted and do not sweat the details, but instead are working primarily on the things you have identified as most important.

The other benefit that you will find is that once you realize your accomplishments, the work and effort it took to get there becomes less and less relevant. Think of it as a labor of love. A mother who gives birth to a new child goes through an unimaginable amount of pain to deliver her new baby. But once that baby is placed into her arms, the pain of childbirth quickly disappears, and all she can focus on, and all she cares about, is that new baby. So it is with achieving new levels of accomplishment for there is no amount of pain that is not overcome by a greater amount of joy at the results of your efforts.

Let me suggest one more analogy to amplify how change is slow and painful until it produces its intended consequences. This is relevant to the thought of getting there versus arriving. Imagine that you are planning for the vacation of a lifetime. Maybe it's a honeymoon or a trip to celebrate your twenty-fifth wedding anniversary. Think of the hours of planning, saving, researching, and booking that you do to ensure that no detail is left undone, and there is no room for error. We've all done something like this. Likely, you planned for this trip for months, maybe even longer, certainly more than sixty-six days, incidentally.

In addition to the planning, there is the trip itself. There are probably several hours of travel involved, and you will need to carry everything you need to ensure that all is perfect when you get there. The point is, with all of the buildup, planning, and travel required to get there, you can sometimes wear yourself out before you even arrive. But the moment you arrive and see that city, look at that mountain, smell that ocean breeze, or walk into that resort—all is forgotten. Every sense in your body is filled with the joy of arriving, and no matter how long it took and how much it costs, you can't imagine having not done what was needed to get there.

And so, my friends, it is with change. It's a slow, arduous process. But the rewards for yourself and quite likely many others are well worth the effort.

No magic, just consistency.

I've got some bad news for some of you. When you're trying to grow, you can't change nature, and you can't rush the process. There are no magic tricks or shortcuts. You need to do what must be done every day, day after day, until eventually many days breed success. It's just that simple. And just that hard, requiring slow, steady, consistent effort. It's what separates dreamers from achievers.

Half of the battle is just showing up. Many people intend to show up but never quite get there. Or they start but soon fall away. I am always amazed and somewhat amused at what happens at fitness centers at the beginning of the year. They are busy places full of activity, but when a new year dawns, suddenly, there is nowhere to park, the machines are all occupied, and the classes are all full. Nevertheless, those who are there consistently know they just have to ride it out for a couple of weeks, and everything will resume to normal. It's kind of sad really, but half of the challenge in making a change is to not give up and consistently show up every day.

I will take it a step further and say that once you've shown up, go ahead and show out, too. I'm not talking about beating your chest and trying to draw attention to yourself. I'm talking about once you show up, go ahead and do your best. Be different. Be better. So many people are just going through the motions. Whether it's at work, home, or even volunteering. But there are some who show out, and the people who show out can be spotted a mile away. They are not only there, but they're throwing a party while they're at it. They're happy, they're engaged, and their electricity puts a charge into other people.

Those really seeking to make a significant impact on their culture push boundaries also. Not in a bad way, but in a way that challenges other people to consider their widely held beliefs or what is the 'norm' according to society. These people color outside the lines and think outside of the box. They are the people who really affect change by impacting others around them. I am convinced that their formula is simple. They ask the question, *why?* over and over again. A lot of people ask the question once, get the stock answer and shrug their shoulders and move on; whereas, people who make real, effective change keep asking why, until they discover something that would have been otherwise left uncovered. So, again, no matter what your situation or the task ahead of you, I encourage you to become a person who asks why enough times to instill a new what, or how.

If you are planning to create a huge tree, I encourage you to become a master of your schedule. The reason is I find that people who do not schedule their time usually end up getting it filled by unimportant tasks. As mentioned in the last section, as a minimum, you should schedule three prioritized activities every day. To do this effectively, you should plan those activities the night before. Otherwise, you open yourself to one of those days where you look at the clock and realize it's 4:00 and all you've accomplished all day is a lot of busywork. And to truly master your schedule, you should be working on quarterly, monthly, and weekly goals. If you want to become the type of high achiever who makes significant change, you must master your schedule, and work diligently on your highest priorities.

Finally, as you develop a focused plan, you should also be planning for success. Your mental mindset when it comes to change, growth, and accomplishment is key. You must believe that you are capable of change before change will occur. I have transformed myself a number of times over the last few years, and I recommend two practices that have been invaluable in aiding me to do so: visualization and meditation.

Meditation enables me to be open to new ideas, new thoughts, and new experiences. Visualization helps me to see what I would look like after I have already achieved my desired outcomes. I do not profess to be an expert at either activity, but I can certainly attest to the fact that these two tools significantly increase your chances of success.

Now that you are ready to put in the work, plan for the work ahead, and grow your seeds into significance, it's time to look at the mountain-moving results that you will achieve, which we'll cover in the next chapter.

FOR REFLECTION
THREE MOUNTAIN-MOVING IDEAS

- Take what you believe is your most significant goal. Assuming you haven't, take time to evaluate and break that goal down to quarterly, monthly, weekly, and daily steps that will ensure your success.

- What three things do you need to make into daily habits? Start tomorrow and track them for sixty-six days in a journal or on an app on your phone.

- Make a list each month of everything you have accomplished in the past thirty days and also what you need to accomplish in the next thirty. evaluate these lists quarterly and annually to set goals for the future and stretch yourself even further.

CHAPTER 9

MOUNTAIN-MOVING RESULTS

*"May your trails be crooked, winding,
lonesome, dangerous, leading to the most
amazing view. May your mountains
rise into and above the clouds."*

EDWARD ABBEY, AUTHOR

Congratulations! You have done the work, you have accomplished the goals, you're getting somewhere, and now your view is changing. Not just the view of yourself, but the way you view others, the way you view opportunity, and the way you view your beliefs. The path to success takes a lot of hard work, and a lot of fortitude. I ask you to consider whether luck plays a part because I believe that luck is what I call serendipity and that God has placed me exactly where He wants me to be. But we'll debate on that later.

No matter how you got here, you have arrived. Now the question is, what are you going to do? Are you going to bask in the glory and take all the credit for yourself? Are you going to continue to climb to higher elevations? And, most importantly, are you going to share your success with others? We'll spend this chapter talking about what's next.

Sacrifice and paying the price for significance.

Now that you've arrived, you should celebrate your arrival as quickly and quietly as possible, and then move on. I do not say this to diminish your accomplishments or your pride, but I say this because of an awareness that all of us have a tendency to lose focus once we reach a mountain peak and then inevitably slide backward. I compare this to being on a fad diet. Anyone can lose twenty pounds, but can you consistently keep it off? Because if you don't stay committed to the changes you've made, you're just as likely to fall backward.

Additionally, rather than enjoy the fruits of your labor alone, you need to share your success and the spoils of it with others. It's a lot more fun to bring people along with you once you've reached the top of the mountain rather than climbing alone and having no one to share it with. This brings up the first principle from this chapter: it's only significant if it's shareable. Sure, you can accumulate many great and wonderful things for yourself. You can take pride in, covet, and collect all of your little trinkets along the way. The person who said, *"It's lonely at the top,"* was right. Especially if you're all alone when you get there.

It is a far different view from the mountain if you can share your accomplishments with others. Primarily, there are two groups of people you can share it with. First are the people who helped get you there and supported you along the way. Showing appreciation is a sure character trait of people who are culture-changing. In fact, it's almost a necessity if you plan to lead anyone else besides yourself. Second, and most importantly, are the people who will benefit most from your charitable giving activities. If you have never been much for giving to, or working with, charities, I cannot encourage you enough to start. In all of my charitable work, I have not come across one person who was not thankful or appreciative of even the smallest kindness.

Just as equal to the joy you will discover in helping and serving others is how you will feel while doing it. It is not an exaggeration to say it is life-changing. And undertaking charitable actions in a group changes everyone's lives and the dynamics within the group. There are many team-building exercises available, but I assure you that there is no greater way to build team unity and camaraderie than by working together on a charitable project.

These activities require a bit of humility and getting outside of your comfort zone. It is not always easy, but it's always worth it. I would encourage you to adopt the mindset of being a mirror and not a window. Think of yourself as a reflection to all other people of what you have gained, what you have accomplished, and what you have to share. If others do not see themselves reflected in your image, then you haven't yet humbled yourself enough and done the things that really matter. The other benefit of being a reflection and not a window is that these actions take the focus off of yourself and shine a light on others. Literally and figuratively. The more you reflect the light and the successes you have collected along your journey, the more others will be inspired by your efforts and strive to better themselves.

To state the obvious, the more wisdom you earn on your way to the top of the mountain, the more you will have to share once you arrive. Of course, the harder you work, typically the more you make or get. But it is also true that the harder you work, the more you appreciate what you have and the more you are willing to sacrifice yourself to help others. It is also true that the more you share, the greater your desire will grow to share more. This may seem counterintuitive, but it has rung true in my own life. It is not an easy place to get to, but it is a wonderful place to be. If there is a better definition of joy and fulfillment, I have not yet found it.

Most importantly, the journey to the top is not about you. If that news is disappointing or disheartening, I'm sorry, but I believe the best people in the world are the ones who are focused on other people. Sure, we all have needs, desires, goals, and dreams, but it is so much more rewarding and fulfilling to share those personal victories with other people. Some folks are just naturally able and naturally gifted to acquire and achieve great things all by themselves. But just because they can do it alone does not mean they should keep it only for themselves. There are many broken people who have achieved unlimited worldly success. My suggestion to you is that you should make your life more about who it is being done with than what you are getting. For example, the question to ask yourself is: *who have you benefited?* rather than, *what have you earned?*

> **Not the size of the faith, but the size of the God.**

A warning to all skeptical readers: this section is about God, our relationship with Him, and how great and big He is. You are welcome to move on to the next section of the book, but I encourage you to read on because there are some great lessons for all of us contained herein. Again, my intention is not to try and 'convert' you or brainwash you. Rather, I simply wish to pass on the message that being a Christian, as I understand it, means that I should not only love and respect all people, but share valuable insights and lessons with them.

Some might say that the future is not very bright. There are wars, hatred, bigotry, misogyny, racism, and corruption. I am not interested in adding politics to that list. Given all that, it is not easy to be optimistic or opportunistic in today's world. And if you think you are, or can be, there are plenty of people around to convince you otherwise. My advice to you is to look backward before you look forward. Look at all of the things that you have accomplished, look at all of the times when it seemed there was no way you could get through the day, but somehow you did. As a Christian, I have the assurance that God has led me to where I am now. Rest assured, I have had plenty of heartaches and setbacks in my life, but nonetheless, God has been faithful and brought me through them all relatively unscathed. I have even found favor with others and accomplished a number of things of which I am very proud.

Therefore, before I look forward, not knowing what lies ahead and considering all of the uncertainties, I look back and see the path I have traveled. This brings me comfort, it brings me courage to face tomorrow, and it brings me joy for the growth I have experienced. And I am then motivated to move forward, because the same God who was with me yesterday is with me today and will go before me tomorrow, leading me down the path he has chosen for me for the rest of my life. That's something I get excited about!

Likewise, when I consider all of the hardships I have had to endure, I realize that my burdens aren't really that challenging. In fact, even in my darkest days, I recognize that He lifted me up. He did all of the heavy lifting so that I could rest and be restored in Him. Some of you may scoff and disagree with my approach, but you cannot discount how it has impacted my life and why it has led me to write this book. I am not just referring to tragic circumstances either. Sometimes we endeavor to undertake projects or goals that seem impossible when we start out. I have proven to myself that if the goal is worthwhile enough, and if it is God's will that this is my path, then the mountain is not insurmountable.

There are two tools that I use to help me remain grounded, centered, and connected with God. One of them I have already mentioned: meditation. I meditate every morning to level-set my thoughts and intentions for the day. This helps me to approach difficult situations and people with a sense of calm assurance, enabling me to remain on an even keel when faced with challenges.

I listen more than I speak, and ask questions to ascertain the emotions behind them. This is a practice I highly recommend.

The other and most powerful tool I have is prayer. I could write a book on this subject, but I will limit my thoughts here. Quite simply, there is not a more powerful tool to ensure a positive mindset. Prayer has all of the benefits of meditation with the added benefit of drawing yourself closer to the creator of the universe. This is hard to explain if you do not believe in or participate in prayer, but I would certainly encourage you to give it a try. I challenge you to participate with an open mind—you will be better off than when you started.

Finally, when considering how big our God is, I urge you to become a big dreamer and challenge yourself to see beyond your present circumstances and capabilities. I highly recommend that you get a notebook and start journaling about everything and anything that you ever wanted to accomplish. If God tells you that you can move mountains with faith as small as a mustard seed, then imagine what you might do with a lot more faith. Getting back to the multiplication effect I mentioned earlier in the book—there is no better example and nothing more exciting than the following equation:

BIG FAITH X BIG DREAMS X BIG GOD = UNLIMITED OPPORTUNITIES

If you take anything away from this book, I hope that it is an insatiable desire to dream and carry out God-sized goals that challenge you to stretch yourself farther than you ever thought possible.

This is not a prosperity message.

Before moving on to the final section, I want to insert a very important caveat to ensure that no one comes away from this chapter with the idea that this is a prosperity message. I am not a fan or a follower of the prosperity gospel movement, which essentially teaches that if you follow Christ, all of your problems will disappear, and you can pray, believe, or give your way out of any circumstance. There are many genuine people in the world who do a lot of good, but it is a discredit to our faith when people use the gospel message to pad their own or other people's pockets.

My focus in writing this book is to portray the message that the most important thing you can do in your life is to give of yourself to others. Be a lover, not a fighter. Bring an olive branch and not a sword. Our culture, our country, our world needs people who care more about blessing others than praising themselves. This requires a switch in mindset from accumulation to distribution. It's having the ability and desire to attain many wonderful things but then acting as a conduit to pass them on to other people. This is the same message that Jesus brought to the world 2,000 years ago, and the message is still as relevant today. And, boy, does the world need to hear it.

I challenge you to start focusing on how you can give more than you can get. This message should be given the serious consideration it deserves. Because the more we get, the more we want; the more we want, the more focused we become on ourselves and not others. Look around you. In your home, in your office, in your neighborhood. What unnecessary things are sitting there idly wasting away? How could you use or repurpose those things to benefit someone else? If you look closely, you'll find a lot. I suggest you put those things to good use by giving them away and blessing others with your abundance.

Rather than prosperity, I encourage you to live a genuine and sincere lifestyle. And, if you really want to live in a way that changes people's perception and lives, I refer you to Paul's list of the fruits of the Spirit in Galatians 5:22–23 which refers to: love, joy, peace, patience, kindness, goodness, faithfulness, gentleness, and self-control. Paul sums this up pretty well, especially when after the list he cites, *"Against such things there is no law."* Use these tools to change your thoughts and change your world.

Finally, to dispel any hint of prosperity, many, if not most, of the things I am talking about directly relate to money or possessions. The story of the widow with one mite in the Bible is a wonderful example of someone who earned the praise of Jesus not because of the value of how much she gave, but rather the value she placed on who she was giving it to by giving everything she had. God does not put a price tag on how much we give. In fact, there are many verses in the Bible criticizing and rebuking people with money. I am not aware of any passages that rebuke the poor.

My point is you can't put a price tag on a relationship with God any more than you should put a price tag on what you give. With the right attitude, you could give everything you don't need to help others. Those kinds of people change the world.

To close this chapter, it is important to note that these things must be done in a way that preserves your personal character and integrity. To the detriment of my marriage and young children, I personally spent many years of my career focused only on achieving my business goals. I cannot go back and relive those days, but I can encourage you not to make the same mistake. Stay connected to those closest to you, no matter what you're doing or where you are going. The world does not need any more self-made people whose private lives are in shambles. Well-rounded people develop great business, personal, financial, spiritual, physical, and marital health. Not only do they seem to excel at everything they do, but they are also successful with relationships. They especially excel at having positive marriages and positive kids in a world that needs a lot more examples of both. My point is, to live a life of significance, you have to succeed in all phases of life. Otherwise, while you may succeed at a few things, you may be sacrificing others that may create regrets later in life. And no one wants to live with regrets; they should only regret they don't have more time.

FOR REFLECTION
THREE MOUNTAIN-MOVING IDEAS

- Whom can you share your success with and How? What do you need to do today?

- In what area(s) of your life do you need to dream bigger? What have you always dreamed of accomplishing?

- In what ways and in what areas of your life do you need to start giving more than getting?

SECTION 4

WORKING
AND CHANGING

CHAPTER 10

YOUR CURRENT REALITY

*"I made an assessment of my own life, and
I began to live it. That was freedom."*

FERNANDO FLORES, ENGINEER AND POLITICIAN

As we dive into the final section of the book, I hope to encourage people of all creeds, colors, and religions to take stock of their lives and consider uniting us all together rather than splitting us apart. In this chapter, we will consider the mindset needed to either gain or maintain this goal. As we have discussed throughout, it is well worth the time and trouble to become a person who makes a significant impact on your small corner of the world.

Slow down, sit still, stay focused.

All of us lead busy, hectic lives. Our culture demands that we do more, faster. The harried pace at which most of us live our lives is neither sustainable nor healthy. In fact, it can be argued that it is a prominent cause of the hostility that exists in our society today. We not only live but we listen in sound bites, just waiting to hear something that will set us off or send us into a frenzy. I want to suggest that to be successful and to change your current reality, it is going to require a massive shift in your current *modus operandi*.

You can call me old or old-fashioned and you will be right on both accounts, I suppose. I long for the days before electronics invaded our heads, our hands, and our hearts. A time when we were much better at living in the moment and really and truly communicating with other people. I truly wonder how much productivity, affinity, and intimacy we are sacrificing in all of our relationships because of how distracted we have become by the pervasiveness of technology.

I am not attempting to put the genie back in the bottle, because technology and smartphones are here to stay. But I am appealing to you to focus on the art of becoming a better listener. The better you listen, the better you will understand; and the better you understand, the more constructively you can act and react to what is going on around you. I am not so old-fashioned that I am questioning the amount of learning available from today's technology. I believe that there is a unique opportunity available for people who are willing to genuinely interact with other human beings. People that are willing to listen to and understand others before taking action solely focused on themselves is becoming completely counter-culture.

As a Christian, I believe it is my duty to be a person who reaches out to, and connects with, other people. Not in a confrontational way, but in a way that brings connectivity and enables a sense of community, regardless of religions or world views. As His disciple, I believe one of God's expectations of me is to reach out to others. There are countless scriptures in the New Testament to support this view. If my faith is real, it has to make a difference in the way I think, the way I act, and the way I interact with others. The other truth is that if my faith is real and genuine, it will be noticed—not as someone attempting to draw attention to themselves, but as someone who is acting different and making a difference.

The other benefit of taking time to consider our lives, our motives, and our direction is that it takes our focus from where we are to where we want to be. It also allows us to see beyond the way things are today and to visualize how they might be in the future. So many people today are reactionary and not progressive in their thinking. Which is a shame considering we are a very creative species, and I fear we are getting farther and farther away from using those innate abilities. Our future and the future of those around us, are only limited by how much we limit ourselves. Of course, there comes a time when you have to act, and the challenge I perceive in our culture today is that we're not spending enough time daydreaming. I fear the exact opposite is true.

The great thing about thoughtful planning *and* daydreaming is that the goal becomes far less important than the process. What do I mean by that? I mean that the better we plan, the more likely that our plans and intentions are realized and we make the big changes that we aspire to make. The bonus of all this, is that while you're doing all of the thinking, dreaming, and planning, you're putting those ideas into action, and you are becoming the person you aspire to become as you work through the process. That said, I caution you not to become so focused on achievement that you lose sight of who you become in the process.

Many years ago, I went through an Executive MBA program at Baylor University. It was one of those programs where you went to class all day on Friday and Saturday twice per month, and then worked in between weeks for two years. All while maintaining a full-time job. It was an arduous process, to say the least, but one that eventually earned me an MBA that I am very proud to own. I mention this to share a point that one of my professors made over and over again as I went through his class: When our entire class would be stressed out and ready to freak out, he would always say, *"Guys, relax, it's the journey."* It took me a long time to realize that Dr. Sam Seamen was right. We need to do a much better job of slowing down and enjoying the journey. Thanks, Sam.

How to benefit others.

If our focus is to truly shift from ourselves to others, this will require some very deep soul searching and significant changes in how we respond to those around us. When I made the determination that I wanted to change my life, I had to realize that I am not the king of anything, especially where, despite my efforts to be in complete control of everything that was going on around me, it was not realistic for me to hold on to such things. As such, there are a few tips I have learned, and I will share them with you now.

The first thing you should do is open your hands. In other words, instead of trying to hold on to everything that you perceive as yours, you must go from a clenched fist to an open hand, as there is no other way to properly serve people. And the truth is, most people are more capable of receiving from us than we give them credit for. Although it was a big adjustment for me, my life got infinitely better and less complicated after I lost my grip on everything and opened up my hands.

The next thing to open is your heart. This was a personal struggle for me. Everyone who struggles with these sorts of issues always feels like they are the only person in the world who has this very personal stigma to overcome, but I have learned that this is rarely the case because many of us build walls around our hearts to protect them from being hurt or harmed. For me, this meant I had a hard time opening up to other people and really expressing my feelings, especially my thoughts. I thought if I didn't have the perfect answer it was better to be quiet than to let others inside my heart. The truth is, as I have discovered, the more you open your heart, the bigger your heart gets. It isn't easy; in fact, sometimes it's downright uncomfortable, but it opens the door to seeing other people as in need of love and encouragement as you are. All of the steps to benefiting others are important, but this message in particular is the key to your future success.

Now that we have talked about what we need to open in order to benefit others, let's talk about a couple of things that you should close. The first and most important thing that needs to be closed is your mouth. My suggestion is that the less you talk and the more you listen, the more you will see opportunities. This is a little tongue in cheek, but I believe that if we use our eyes and our ears significantly more than we use our mouths, we will discover a vast array of opportunities we have never before been aware of. It stands to reason, because typically when we are talking, we are focused on ourselves, conveying our own ideas or thoughts, and working to perceive how others are receiving our message. If we are looking and listening, we are more able to pick up on other people's ideas, and what is important to them, as well as see opportunities from a different perspective.

I challenge all of us to close the gap between affluence and poverty in our country. Certainly, the United States is among the most affluent countries in the world. Nevertheless, data from the census bureau continues to show that nearly forty million people in the United States live below the poverty line. Additionally, it has been suggested that there are as many as another sixty million people living near the poverty line. If these numbers are correct, it means that nearly one-third of the population of the US is in, or near, poverty. These numbers can and must be lowered dramatically in the new millennium. Again, it is beyond the scope of this book to offer suggestions, but many organizations already exist to help combat this dilemma, and many more are waiting to be founded by people of means looking for opportunities to benefit others.

Change your present to give the future a bigger gift.

What do I mean by this? I am talking about leaving a legacy beyond what you will see or experience in your lifetime. I believe that all of us are uniquely gifted with the ability to accept and accomplish this challenge. Why? Because it has been done by many like-minded people who came before us, and did things that we now take for granted, but yet continue to serve people years, decades, and even centuries after their deaths. So, that said, I am challenging you to dream big and sacrifice yourself greatly to produce change that future generations will enjoy. For I believe that being sacrificial is the new norm that we should all shoot for as we build and create ideas, programs, and funds to change the world. I recognize that it's a huge investment of ourselves and others we bring alongside us, but it is this type of sacrificial giving that can change lives and break down barriers between people from different classes and cultures.

While we're dreaming and thinking big, here is a question for you to ponder. How many people in Heaven will know your name? Friend, I realize that 95 percent, if not 99 percent, of us will live our lives in relative obscurity. So, I am not suggesting that we become people who seek accolades. I am suggesting that small segments of the people across our land have the opportunity to impact lives. Imagine if only one person approached you after you got to Heaven and thanked you for what you had done while you were on earth and told you that they would not have gotten there without you. What if it was ten? Or one hundred? Or one thousand? Whether you live in one of the largest cities in America or one of the smallest rural communities, all of us have a chance to make a difference.

I love the goal-setting analogy of setting stretch goals for ourselves. Anyone can set a goal that is easily achievable, but of the small percentage of people who actually set goals, an even more minute amount of the population set goals that stretch them beyond their abilities. I love the thought of setting God-sized goals. Goals that can be achieved and successful only if God is involved in them and seeks to help us accomplish them. Those types of goals, and the people that aren't afraid to set them, excite me, and I hope they excite you, too. Whatever types of things you endeavor to accomplish, I challenge you to go outside of your comfort zone. If all we ever do is shoot layups, life gets pretty mundane. I'd rather try to throw some full-court prayers that get answered every now and then. Even if I only hit the target once.

My fellow dreamers, I will finish this chapter by challenging us all to leave a legacy when we are gone. No matter where you are in life, it is never too soon, or never too late, to start focusing your efforts on the gifts that you can give to others rather than trying to accumulate more for yourself. What can you hand down today that will outlive your personal accomplishments while you're on this earth? I really believe there are many in our society who have the desire to create legacies to leave for future generations. Sure, there are a lot of problems and differences of opinions that we have to overcome, but wouldn't you rather be part of the solution than part of the problem? I hope and pray that in this generation we can reverse the negativity that has overtaken us and shine lights into the darkest and most needy of places. Just as we discussed earlier, planting, nurturing, and growing tiny seeds into substantial trees is not easy, but, as with all things of value, it is worth our best efforts.

FOR REFLECTION
THREE MOUNTAIN-MOVING IDEAS

- What steps and actions can you take to become a better listener? What distractions do you need to eliminate?

- Identify where and how you have clenched hands and walls built around your heart, then develop strategies to let go and tear them down.

- What kind of legacy are you leaving?

CHAPTER 11

THE BRIDGE

"You can't connect the dots looking forward; you can only connect them looking backward. So you have to trust that the dots will somehow connect in your future. You have to trust in something—your gut, destiny, life, karma, whatever. This approach has never let me down, and it has made all the difference in my life."

STEVE JOBS, FORMER CEO, APPLE

In this penultimate chapter, we look at three characteristics that will build bridges between yourself and others. I hope you have been challenged up to this point to employ some of the mountain-moving ideas at the end of each chapter. These are all characteristics exhibited and taught by Jesus and are applicable for all people, not just his followers. His disciples will be living, breathing examples of these characteristics in the flesh for all the world to see. Unfortunately, Christians, as well as every other segment of society, are flawed, sinful people, and we don't always live up to the high expectations of others, and certainly not Jesus.

In the messages of grace, hope, and love, we have the ability to forgive others even when we don't receive those things from them as much as we would like. We all need to hold ourselves to these high standards but be quick to forgive others when they do not. If we can do this, then we will be building bridges and not putting up fences.

Don't say grace, give it.

By definition, grace is freely given, unmerited favor and love. For Christians, we are sinners saved by grace. Grace is not earned, but rather an innate gift. Therefore, we should not fail to give it. One of the many ugly antonyms of grace is neglect. We have neglected decency and dignity to people that are 'different' for far too long. It's past time to set aside our judgmental ways and see people as they really are: flawed people who struggle, but still need and deserve grace. Just like us.

Let's be clear: forgiveness is not a sign of weakness. For far too long, many of us have acted as if it is. We walk around with (several) chips on our shoulders looking for reasons to be angry and unyielding when it comes to other people. And the political world has become one of the most polarizing arenas in our culture. Its effect on us has become so divisive that many families have significant relationship issues based on which party or candidate they support. Mine is one of them. Since one of the tenets of grace is forgiveness, I believe that we need to get over ourselves and recognize that our society is much better off working together than driving a wedge between us.

Briefly, let me emphasize the point that just like so many other things of honor and valor, grace is given and not earned. In other words, the more we give it, the more we get it, and the more we will want to *continue* to give it. I challenge you to try for one day, in every way possible, to offer grace to everyone you come in contact with. See how you feel at the end of that day. From the truck that cuts you off in traffic, to the rude customer you have to deal with at work, to the people you live with who may have had a bad day and want to take it out on you: give grace, not unkindness. I've no doubt your attitude will be significantly improved. So much so, that you will want to go out and do it again and again. Who knows, in sixty-six days or so, you might have just formed a new habit.

Be sure that when you are considering grace that you use equal measurements, as we have a bad tendency to have one set of rules for ourselves and a completely different set of rules for everyone else. What do I mean by this? This is where we are able to easily explain away our own shortcomings, but a similar slip-up from someone else is a different story. Most people, especially the ones you are close to, or live with, are able to see right through this, and if they point out your failings, this can become a point of contention in your most significant relationships. However, others that you are not as close to may not realize that you are behaving in such a manner—not that this excuses the behavior, nor does it alleviate the way people will respond to you negatively because of your judgmental attitude. But, the message is very clear: we cannot have a double standard, where we explain away our own failings and yet criticize others for theirs.

To summarize, the best way to think about getting past the double standard, just as with any other act of kindness, is that you should apply the Golden Rule. Jesus quoted the Golden Rule from Leviticus, in Matthew 7 when he said, *"Do unto others as you would have them do unto you."* This is likely one of the most quoted and well-known verses of scripture in the secular world. But, if it is so pervasive in our culture, then why are we doing such a poor job of implementing it?

This simply should not be. To be able to properly give grace, we must have a heart of compassion for others and develop a mindset of not thinking of ourselves more highly than we do anyone else. Therefore, although the Golden Rule may be well known in our society, I believe it is poorly implemented. I strongly encourage you to take time to think and reflect, while seriously considering what you need to do in order to be able to 'do unto others.' Imagine what an incredible bridge that would build if we elevated others to new heights and encouraged them to cross over from where they are to where they need to be.

Hope builds strength and desire.

Just as with grace, hope is something that you need to have and also can give. Unlike grace, which, in a theological sense, is freely given, hope is something that has to be attained and learned by our own efforts. It is not given, and you don't have to look too closely at other people to determine if they are hope-filled people or not. Usually the answer is written all over their faces, or their attitude and body language give it away anyway. Those who are filled with hope are equally as easy to spot. They have a smile on their faces, their heads are held high, and they have a pep in their step. They greet you with a hearty hello, a firm handshake, and often a pat on the back for good measure. Hopeful people are able to see a bright future no matter what is going on around them. People without hope are usually more focused on what's going on around them and on problems and situations over which they have no direct control.

Attaining and hanging on to hope requires a deep mental and emotional commitment. It cannot just be absorbed into your psyche. Whereas grace is an unmerited favor, generally granted by God, hope is a characteristic like honesty, humility, and kindness. As such, it must be learned, nurtured, and grown into our lives.

Think about people you really admire. Their demeanor never seems to change, and their attitude is always positive. What do you think of when you think of these people? You either want to be more like them, or you want to spend more time with them.

They brighten your day, and make you become present in the moment as well as make you forget about any challenges you may be facing. Sadly, there are far too few people like this in the world. And that's a shame.

What the world needs, and what we need, are more hopeful people to elevate us to new levels so that we can, in turn, elevate others. I have some very good news for you: most people who live their lives with hope love to spend time with other people that feel and act the same way. So, if you're looking to become a more positive and upbeat person, start spending more time with those people who already are. You will be glad you did, and they will be happy to introduce you to their friends.

Here, we come back to the theory of multiplication. For, once you become a hopeful person yourself, you are able to convert others by spreading the message of hope to them. The old saying, *"Smile, and the world smiles with you,"* really rings true. I have witnessed people's entire demeanors and mindsets change simply through the act of smiling at them. Not everyone responds positively because it's a little unusual, but the benefits still outweigh the disadvantages.

My challenge for you to undertake with this concept is this: many of us spend a good amount of time each morning preparing ourselves to look our best. We shower, apply cosmetics and toiletries, and dress to impress. I suggest you add one small accessory to your morning ritual—don't leave home without a smile on your face. People will notice, people will smile back, and it's entirely possible that you'll make someone's day. And regardless of whether you do or you don't, there is a very good chance that you will make yours.

In my opinion, there is no better or more important a gift I can give to others than a message of hope. Especially with all of the rancor and negativity in our society today. Hope can raise people out of their current situations, give them a reason to start down a new path, and change the course of their destinations. Hope can break down walls. Walls of hatred, discrimination, disagreement, and judgment. It can unite people under its cause and allow them to break free from social, sexual, and societal stereotypes.

If you make it your mission to become a champion of hope, you will become a hero to countless others who need more people to give them one of the best gifts they could ever receive. A message that no matter where you are, what you've done, and where you're going, shows them that hope can change their mindset and set them on a new course for success and significance. Let's close this section by focusing on how important it is for people to have a vision for the future. As wise King Solomon said in the book of Proverbs in the Old Testament, *"Where there is no vision, the people perish."*

Everyone wants to have a goal to shoot for, a task to accomplish, or, at a minimum, a reason to live. To the many marginalized people in our society, all they need is a glimmer of hope with the possibility that it could turn into a bigger vision. Many times, for all of us, our vision becomes clearer as we begin to work or pursue a dream. The hardest part is starting, and the best thing we can do for other people is to give them a small nudge by giving them a sliver of hope. I am an admitted optimist, so forgive me if my thoughts seem too simplistic; however, I believe that anyone and everyone can arrive at amazing destinations if they are just given the tools to get there, and a road map to find their way. All of us have gifts to push people in a positive, hope-filled direction. Someone did it for me. Someone may have done it for you. It is our responsibility to pay it forward.

I have never forgotten the words of a former two-term president, during his inaugural run for office. During the 1992 Democratic Convention in New York, then-governor Bill Clinton uttered one of his more famous quotes. *"I still believe in a place called Hope."* So do I, Mr. President.

The world needs love, now.

I saved the best for last. I believe the world would be a much better place if grace and hope were bound all together and tied up in a nice, neat bow by love. Love means so many things in today's world. I have amused myself many times in the past by imagining an alien coming to Earth and asking me to explain what love means. I imagine him in an exasperated tone saying, *"You humans confuse me. You say you love your spouse, but you also say you love your phones. You say you love your children, but you also love spending money on things that don't last. You say you love God, but you also love chocolate. Please explain!"* Our alien friend makes some good points.

In no way am I going to endeavor to define what love is and what it isn't. I know it when I see it, I know it when I feel it, I know it when I share it, and I know it when I see what it can do. But even I would have a hard time explaining it, as I think most of us would. So, rather than endeavor to define love, let's talk about what love does. Ah, now we're getting somewhere because love can do many wonderful things.

Love changes biases. That is to say, love is blind. It does not look at someone's skin, gender, bank account, or clothes. It's just love, and that's what it does. And that being the case, love simply sees people not as they are, but as who they can be. This is not to imply that we should use it as manipulation, rather I suggest that we simply see people as they are—or perhaps better stated, as God sees them. Let's be clear that if God hates all sin, and mine is no better or worse than anyone else's, then this means that He also loves everyone just the same without any bias or filters. And this is also how He asks us to love others when He says, *"Love, as I have loved you."* That is not a suggestion, by the way. Let love do its amazing work and overcome your biases. It's a bridge that everyone should cross.

Next, love destroys poverty. Well, maybe not directly, but it certainly has the ability when manifested through enough individuals who love unconditionally and are just as concerned with loving other people as well as they love themselves. Love sees need. Love sees opportunity. And, yes, love sees hope where others have none or have simply given up. The world is full of wonderful organizations that benefit others, but anyone associated with these organizations would tell you that there is always more that they could do, and more people that they could serve, if they had the additional resources and the extra people to help. My friends, if you are loving well, you will be seeking opportunities to share that love through both your time and your resources. I believe that this is our calling, this is our mission, and this is our duty as a nation to share resources for the benefit of the greater good.

Love drives out hate. I could start and end the paragraph right there. The antithesis of love is hatred, as where love exists, hate cannot. There are too many places in our society where we have allowed hatred in all of its forms and functions to invade our culture and take the place of love. This simply cannot be. We must fight to win back these relationships over self-righteousness. This must be a grassroots effort where we all take up the challenge to reverse the negativity and vitriol that dominate our conversations today.

There is much going on in my circle of influence right now that I am not happy about. I can allow myself to blend in with the majority that would rather perpetuate negativity and anger or become a game-changer who, with love as my backdrop, makes real, effective, lasting change.

Finally, love changes lives. In love, we create our children. In love, we raise and nurture our children. And in love, we send them out into the world. This is the natural order of things. But somehow, the love we give often becomes unsatisfying, and our kids may look to other sources for love. Tragically, these sources sometimes produce negative consequences that they-and we could never have imagined, such as where they end up impoverished, addicted, or emotionally and financially bankrupt due to the choices they make.

So, what does any of this have to do with love and changing lives? If we are to help those in need, only love can bring them back. If we are to make restitution with a group of people that we have disparaged in any way, or judged because of any type of difference between them and us, only love can break down those barriers. If we are to build bridges that will take us from where we are to a better and brighter future, we must simply love one another. It sounds easy, yet it is not simplistic. There are real issues and real detachments in our society that will take a superhuman effort to eradicate. The solutions would need to defy logic and explanation—sounds a lot like love to me.

Therefore, dear reader, our world is in dire need of bridge builders. People who are willing to change the world as it is to create a world that is vastly different. Indeed, one in which no one can imagine except a small band of devoted people who are committed to the cause with grace, hope, and love as the pillars and foundations of their efforts. Two thousand years ago, such a movement began—and it continues today. More than ever, a similar revolution is needed today. The people that started the first revolution were from all different backgrounds, occupations, ethnic groups, and political and sociological viewpoints. They set aside their differences and changed not only the region where they lived, but the whole world. Yes, the time has come to plan our incomprehensible future.

FOR REFLECTION
THREE MOUNTAIN-MOVING IDEAS

- To whom, and how, will you show grace to someone in your life today? What about the person who is the most difficult to give it to?

- How well are you implementing the 'Golden Rule' daily? Who stands to benefit the most when you improve your efforts?

- How, when, and to whom can you deliver a consistent daily measure of hope?

CHAPTER 12

AN INCOMPREHENSIBLE FUTURE

*"If future generations are to remember
us more with gratitude than sorrow,
we must achieve more than just the
miracles of technology. We must also
leave them a glimpse of the world as
it was created, not just as it looked
when we got through with it."*

LYNDON B. JOHNSON, THIRTY-SIXTH U.S. PRESIDENT

President Lyndon B. Johnson issued the above quote over fifty years ago on September 3, 1964. He used it during a speech in which he introduced the Wilderness Act. And now, global warming is one of the most significant topics of our world today, especially with young people who are concerned about how the world is going to look when they reach the age of their parents. However, I believe that this quote is also significant when we talk about making any kind of improvements for future generations.

Many people never start out with the idea of how things will be left when they are gone, but as they age, these issues become more relevant. Whether you are young or old, you have a role to play now, in building a future that we can all be proud of. The concept of 'leaving it better than you found it' is certainly not new, but it seems to have been cast aside in favor of the notion of accumulating 'everything, all the time.' If we want to leave a glimpse of the world as it was created, it's time for all of us, regardless of age, to start thinking that our time is short. Because it is. Returning to our parable about the mustard seed—it is of paramount importance that we all start planting seeds today that grow into large, sustainable trees tomorrow. For our sakes, and for the sakes of those who come after us.

What will your tree look like?

Just like people, trees come in all shapes and sizes, and no two are exactly alike. Some grow to tremendous heights, encompassing majestic branches and limbs with thousands of leaves; others are very small in stature and have limited capabilities to provide shade or security. Some trees are also tremendously healthy, and others are very sick. The person who plants a tree has a significant ability to determine the health of the tree. In fact, these arborists could plant and grow many trees that become great sources of benefit to everything around them, and everything they touch.

When metaphorically looking at our lives as a tree, consider the reality that there is no one like you. This is an important point. For example, if you were created to do only what you can accomplish, and if you don't do your part, you are not completely fulfilling your intended reason for being. You could become a small tree, hidden in a tiny garden with little chance for growth or significance, but the world will miss out on what you could have been, had you become all you were meant to be. For you are uniquely gifted to achieve things that no one else but you can do.

Friend, I want to encourage you to do your part, to live your life to the fullest, and to be everything that you can be, for your benefit and the benefit of everyone around you. No matter what you choose to do or where you choose to do it, you have a part to play, and the world is waiting to see you sprout up from where you are and become something a lot bigger than you imagined you could be. If we individually all played a part in our own stories by striving to make the world a better place to live, soon communities, cities, states, and our country would be unrecognizable as scores of people begin to rise up and define a more positive, inclusive, and loving society. The future would look increasingly promising.

As mentioned previously, if you are going to plant your tree, some planning is in order. Assessing your passions, skills, abilities, and values will give you a picture of what you can do. There are many unfilled needs in our country that need passionate, committed people to step up and distend them. There are also limitless opportunities to join forces with existing groups, clubs, and charitable organizations where you could put your skills to work and help them fulfill their mission and goals. Most likely, there are countless openings in a community near you.

Perhaps your skills and abilities would call you to travel to another city or state to best apply them. Whatever the case, your challenge is to find the best place to plant yourself based upon the intersection of needs and capabilities. Just as a tree needs to be planted in fertile soil with the right amount of sunlight, shade, and water, so you need to put yourself in a place that will give you the best chance to make the most significant impact. And don't necessarily jump at the first opening or need you see. Rather, take your time and find the place where you can make the most impact.

After you have determined the place where you will plant and grow yourself, just like a tree once it has begun to take root, I recommend that you use all of your resources and efforts to grow and provide shade and a safe place to land for all the people around you. As people begin to rest in, and under, your tree, your significance will grow, and you will be able to branch out and grow to even greater heights and cover more ground than you could ever have imagined. Perhaps you can use the seeds from your mature tree to plant new trees and make an even brighter future for others.

Friend, no matter where or how you plant, only you are uniquely capable to do what only you can do. When you have fulfilled your destiny, the world and its future generations will be grateful.

Writing your obituary.

I want to leave you with the encouragement and truth that your life matters. And so do the lives of others who benefit from yours. I hope this book has challenged you to make a difference in your world. My sincere hope after you finish this book is that you get active and get involved in breaking down walls and changing the world. I hope some of my messages have resonated with you, and you are ready to change the way you live your life so that others in need will have their lives changed, too. I encourage you to think ahead to the end of your life and what you want it to look like because none of us are promised tomorrow. If you have a 'someday' list, you must either commit to do it, or forget it, as the fact is, someday may never come, and today is all you have. And, if you are not putting everything you have into each day, I fear you may end up at the end of your life with more regrets than accomplishments. For me, this means that on my deathbed, I want to be proud of what I did, not sorry for what I didn't do.

As you may have picked up in this book, I am a bit of a sports fan. Notice I didn't say baseball or football, just sports. There are some sports I am more interested in than others, but, by and large, if it involves competition and someone is keeping score, I'm in. There is one sports analogy that has become fairly trite over the last several years, but it is still true and has more meaning than most athletes realize. Many times, you will hear coaches or players say,

"Leave it all out on the field." The way it is used is a noble enough gesture, but I wonder if they really mean it, or if that's just what they think they're supposed to say? When it comes to life and death, and what lies in between the beginning and end of yours, then 'leaving it all out on the field' should be how we live our lives every day.

To me, this statement means that we should do our best each and every day. It doesn't mean we'll be guaranteed to always be successful, but it does mean that we should always show up and put forward our best efforts. Just like an athlete, when our daily 'game' is over, we may be used up and worn out, but how satisfying would it be to know that you had given your best and that, as encouraged in the Bible, *"whatever your hands have found to do that day, you did it with all of your might"*? Therefore, if you start each day with the intention to leave it all on the field, I am convinced that you will leave a legacy that you will be proud of, and others will benefit from, for generations to come.

I would also like to encourage you from another sports standpoint. Whether you are in the first quarter of your life, or the fourth quarter and time is running out, set your mind on finishing well. Maybe the game up to this point has been a complete failure, but you still have time to finish on a high note and leave yourself, your fans, and, yes, even the opposing team and their fans, with the image of someone who finished well. No one remembers the batter who struck out every time they batted in the game if he comes up in the ninth inning and hits the game-winning home run! They only remember that you won the game. And so it is with life. As long as you have breath, you have a chance to finish well and leave a lasting image of success and accomplishment. It's never too late to start, and it's always too soon to give up. Step into the batter's box and take your best swing.

Let's shift our focus and talk about investing for the future. Any financial professional will tell you that the earlier you start investing, the more dividends you will have when you reach retirement. And, so it is with investing in others and giving yourself in a charitable and sacrificial manner. The sooner you start, the more you will have to show for it. Wherever you are in your life cycle, and whatever you invest in today, over time it will provide greater returns and opportunities for further investments. Even if you aren't here to enjoy them, your heirs will enjoy the benefits. As we discussed earlier in the book, think of everyone as your neighbor and your heir. Make an investment today that they will benefit from in the future.

To conclude, I want to address the multiplication concept one more time in terms of leaving a legacy that will last well beyond our time on the planet. If what you do today impacts one person, I believe we would call that endeavor a success. If the next day, it impacted two people, we would start to get really excited. If the number of people continued to double each day, at the end of one month, your investment would have impacted almost 5.4 million people. This is not speculation on my part. It is simple math and, specifically, multiplying your efforts each day by a factor of double.

Isn't that incredible?! Who wouldn't want to make that type of investment? How much better shape would our country and our world be in if people became more devoted to making investments? Okay, maybe the law of diminishing returns sets in, and instead of 5.4 million, you only impact one million? Or maybe it's only half that or 10 percent of that? I think it would be safe to say that when they wrote your obituary, that despite what you might have done up until now, you will still be remembered as someone who impacted the present and future generations in ways that could never be imagined. That is the kind of impact I want you to have. If you begin this process today, the future will indeed be unimaginable in a positive way. And it's not wishful thinking; it's multiplication.

FOR REFLECTION
THREE MOUNTAIN-MOVING IDEAS

- What unique gifts, talents, and passions do you possess that you can use to bless others?

- What specific actions will this book inspire you to make? write them down now.

- Consider what you will do now so that at the end of your life you have no regrets.

MY MOMENT OF TRUTH –THE REAL REASON FOR THIS BOOK

"You can preach a better sermon with your life than with your lips."

OLIVER GOLDSMITH, NOVELIST

I want to close with a genuine and heartfelt message that I hope inspires you. I also hope it makes you angry and makes you take action. Dr. Martin Luther King said, *"When I am angry, I can pray well and preach well."* Therefore, I hope to close this book by revealing my heart and hope to all.

First, I struggled as I considered writing this book. I started and stopped a few times. I am a white, aging, conservative, southern, Christian, Republican male. That affords me certain luxuries that others do not receive and makes it difficult for me to empathize with people who are facing struggles because of their gender, race, religion, or political standing. I am also, like Dr. King, angry about what is happening in my country today. All the division, derision, and disrespect for human beings across our entire country makes me want to make changes. But before I launch into that, let me backup and tell you about my journey to write this book.

As I mentioned in the introduction, I have always had a desire to write. When I finally made the decision to jump in and do it, I had just decided to retire from my wholesale women's shoe business of thirty-three years. Along with my brother, I was the family's second-generation owner. My company had been my life for the last thirty-three years, but I had also worked there with my dad since I was ten, helping him to pack shoes and ship them to customers and then began selling with him at trade shows as a young teen.

During my career, I had the distinct honor and pleasure to work alongside some of the most wonderful people I have ever met. Many of them I have known since I was a child. Therefore, to decide to walk away from the company was a monumental decision, to say the least. And a few years ago, I might have joked I would retire from the company when they carried me out on a stretcher and put me in the hearse. My wife and I had discussed the idea of early retirement for a long time. In recent years, we had similar discussions with my brother.

But not until I began considering pursuing my dream of writing a book did I get a vision of where I wanted to go, and why I thought now was the time to step away. And several months ago, during a time of reading and prayer, God put it on my heart to write a book about the parable of the mustard seed. Just as with any seedling, the idea took some time to germinate in my soul, but as I looked at the things in the world that really bothered me, the vision started to become clearer. I wanted to challenge readers to make life-changing decisions; therefore, I had to carefully consider my own life and determine whether it would line up with what I would be asking others to do. In other words, would I be practicing what I would be preaching?

Let me be very transparent—in no way do I want to represent that I left behind a steady job and risked my entire future on my current journey. I lived very comfortably off my shoe business, and if I never make another dollar in my life, I will still be okay. And this realization is what led me to an even deeper purpose.

I want to see all the injustices in our country come to an end. I am only just starting on my journey, but my intention is to use the wealth I have, and the wealth I may accumulate, to support causes—both financially and personally—by investing in them to lift others out of poverty, need, discrimination, and judgment.

I am placing my trust in God, and the general goodness of people, by donating 100 percent of the proceeds from the sales of this book to charities of my choosing. I also intend someday to start a family foundation that will support causes to elevate people and build bridges to take them from where they are to where they should be. You can read much more about my mission and goals at https://www.eric-harrison.com. It is my hope, prayer, and plea to create a viral movement with this book, to start a revolution. As the more books that are sold, the more people whose lives can be impacted.

I AM A CHRISTIAN. THE END.

*"I believe in Christianity as I believe that
the sun has risen; not only because I see it,
but because by it I see everything else."*

C. S. LEWIS, WRITER

I am compelled to ensure clarity, and I did not dance around it throughout this book. I am a Christian. Period. End of story. That means that I believe Jesus Christ is the only pathway to God the Father.

You see, I believe my job as a Christian is to love everyone. That's what Jesus did during his three-year ministry on earth, and as best as I understand it, that is what he teaches me to do by his words and actions. Nowhere in the Bible am I told to judge other people based on how they live their lives. Jesus never shied away from people, whether outcasts or downtrodden. On the contrary, he went out of his way to interact with them. To my Christian brothers and sisters, I say: stop being a stumbling block. Stop living duplicitous lives and start supporting the very people Jesus is telling us to reach out to. We compromise our faith, our church, and our Father when we act as judge and jury. And this is a problem in the Christian church that needs to stop today.

To the rest of you reading this, no matter whether you believe in another religion or none at all: I want to tell you I am sorry. I am sorry that the Christians around you may not have shown you the love, compassion, and understanding that you deserve. It breaks my heart to think that so much of the criticism against the faith is because of how we have hurt other people.

I also want to say, in anger, that Christians are not the enemy. The treatment that the church is getting in the mainstream press and society today is wrong. The Christian faith that we live under is one of love, humility, and unity. We are not exclusive; we are inclusive. Just as many Christians need to set aside their biases, so do others outside of the church. I can assure you that we are all flawed human beings, and no better than anyone else. But Christians are simply saved by grace and called to extend and speak the same grace to everyone we come in contact with. As I mentioned earlier in the book, we have much more in common than we do differences.

I would like to end this book with a promise and a pledge. I promise that as a Christian, I will love and respect others even if I completely disagree with their beliefs or lifestyles. The truth is, I have no desire to debate with you—I would much rather engage with you. To that end, it is my intention to use this book as a platform, and a pledge, to change the perception of Christians today. I assure you, we are not enemies, and I promise you that I will endeavor to stop others from alienating and start relating.

Acknowledgements

I would like to thank my J. Reneé family, who I had the pleasure and joy to work with and lead every day for thirty-three years. The things we accomplished and the life we shared together will never be forgotten; and the value I received from it can never be repaid. For thirty-three years, you encouraged, inspired, and amazed me, and you always made me look better than I really am.

To the Self-Publishing School team and community: you turned my dreams into reality. To Chandler Bolt, for your enthusiasm, encouragement, and vision. May SPS continue to grow and prosper and encourage more aspiring authors like me to follow their dreams. To my writing coach, Scott Allan (scottallanauthor.com), thank you for believing in me and guiding me on my journey when I had no direction. Your leadership has meant more to me than I can put into words. To everyone else who works for or who is associated with SPS, you made me believe in myself and taught me that in the struggle between faith and fear, the only mistake I can ever make is not trying.

To my mother, Reneé Harrison. You have inspired me in so many ways numerous times during my life. If I am ever down, all I have to do is spend a few minutes with you before I am ready to run through walls again. Your creativity, determination, and drive to do things better than you have to will continue to inspire me for the rest of my life.

To my friends and family who have encouraged me all along the way on this journey, "thank you" does not begin to express my appreciation. To those who have helped me to launch this book and its message, I thank you for your willingness to support me and my causes. Your messages and calls of support and your willingness to share this with your circles of influence I hope and pray will help to influence lives for many years to come.

YOUR **FREE** BONUS GIFTS

As a show of appreciation to my readers,
I am giving away two **FREE** bonus gifts:

Mustard Seed Faith Individual and Small-Group Study Guide

Being Different, Acting Different, and Making a Difference ebook

Both of these are available on my website:
www.eric-harrison.com

About the Author

Eric Harrison has been a salesman his entire life. At the age of ten, he began delivering and selling subscriptions for a local newspaper, and working for his family's wholesale women's shoe company, J. Reneé Group. He worked officially in his family's shoe business for thirty-three years, and the last eleven of these were spent as co-owner and Chief Executive Officer. In 2019, he sold his interest in the business to his partner and brother, Kai, and has now embarked on a journey to encourage and inspire others through writing and speaking his message of *Being Different, Acting Different, and Making a Difference.*

Eric, and his wife, Jennifer, live in Dallas, Texas, and in 2019 they celebrated their thirtieth wedding anniversary. They have three adult children and love to travel and spend time with family and friends.

A Special Invitation

Your feedback on this book would be invaluable. I encourage you to share any and all comments, thoughts, and ideas with me at: feedback@eric-harrison.com.

In addition, I ask that you please rate this book on Amazon, as positive reviews will encourage others to join me on my journey.

This book would not have been possible without the leadership, coaching, and assistance of Self-Publishing School. If you are an aspiring author, or think you have an idea that needs to be heard, I encourage you to learn more and join the SPS community at:

https://self-publishingschool.com

Made in the USA
Monee, IL
01 October 2022

15027328R00070